CAMPAIGN

ALSO BY DAVID BRESKIN

Poetry
DIRTY BABY
Supermodel
Escape Velocity
Fresh Kills

Fiction
The Real Life Diary of a Boomtown Girl

Non-Fiction
Inner Views: Filmmakers in Conversation
We Are The World

As Editor
RICHTER 858

CAMPAIGN

Elective Poems by David Breskin

MadHat Press
Asheville, North Carolina

MadHat Press
MadHat Incorporated
PO Box 8364, Asheville, NC 28814

Copyright © 2017 David Breskin
All rights reserved

The Library of Congress has assigned
this edition a Control Number of
PB: 2017904377
HC: 2017907472

ISBN 978-1-941196-47-2 (paperback)
ISBN 978-1-941196-50-2 (hardcover)

Carbon offsets to neutralize the carbon emissions associated with the production and distribution of this book have been purchased through Carbonfund.org Foundation.

Cover and interior design by David Breskin

www.MadHat-Press.com

First Printing

CAMPAIGN: ADVANCE MEN

"David Breskin is a righteous, exacting, politically astute poet, and his *Campaign* is something truly new, a blend of visionary journalism and poetry's formal fire. Nobody else sounds like him. These poems are speedy and savage, and grimly funny, driven hard by moral insult and the grotesque moment our polity is suffering through. Every one is a little furnace of truth."

—W.S. Di Piero

"There's nothing convenient about these 7-Elevens, and David Breskin's aisles are stocked with fresh, surprising and often brilliant poetic treats, not the usual stale campaign fare. Talk about a fresh angle! These "Elective Poems" may be the only good thing to come out of 2016."

—Jonathan Alter, MSNBC analyst
and author of *The Center Holds: Obama and His Enemies*

"David Breskin's poems incarnate our present retrograde moment with all the onslaught and disjunction of last year's news crawl. But there's nothing crawling here; instead we get sprints, a forward ferocity that may allow us hope for a future while definitely giving us hope for poetry."

—Dean Young

for Donald J. Ruhman

Monday, February 1, 2016

PRIMARY

Neither soybeans nor corn can
lie to themselves. Vegetable
intelligence commands dirt
poor farmers to vote for pants
on fire politicians.
Caucusing Caucasians. Hog
tied pundits squirmish in pools
of *E. coli* adjectives
cast bronze tonsils in foundries
rusted by the biggest banks
of the biggest river there.

Tuesday, February 2, 2016

TRUMPED

*I think I might come here and
buy a farm.* You could see blood
coming out of his eyes, blood
coming out his wherever.
WHO claims Zika shrinks heads grim
like the pert Fox might playing
trickster God. Suits lay three-card
monte. Trumpets call. The all-
purpose room of a Catholic
church does not serve, in Truth, all
purposes. Baby parts. Jeb!

Wednesday, February 3, 2016

RED CITIZENS UNITED

Right To Rise. Conservative Solutions. Believe Again. America Leads. New Day For America. Concerned American Voters. Club For Growth Action. Carly For America. Courageous Conservatives. Our Children's Future. Security Is Strength. Purple. Stand For Truth. Keep The Promise. Baby Got PAC.

duly noted (via OpenSecrets.org):

Right To Rise supports Bush; *Conservative Solutions* supports Rubio; *Believe Again* supported Jindal; *America Leads* supports Christie; *New Day For America* supports Kasich; *Concerned American Voters* supports Paul; *Club For Growth Action* supports ?; *Carly For America* supports Fiorina; *Courageous Conservatives* supports Cruz; *Our Children's Future* supports Carson; *Security Is Strength* supported Graham; *Purple* supports Paul; *Stand For Truth* supports Cruz; *Keep The Promise* supports Cruz; *Baby Got PAC* supports Rubio.

Thursday, February 4, 2016

WHAT IS THE DIFFERENCE BETWEEN BURNT TOAST AND DIAMOND? (a)

Used to be toast was toast. Now
dude or dudette finishing
fourth is toast. Come next week John
or Jeb! or Chris or Carly
cream-cheesed, buttered, rose-petal
jammed with a carbon dusting
of untaxed flat molecules:
burnt. Other flats slip into
sexy gaps of DNA
underwear causing cancer:
so much ballot-box stuffing.

WHAT IS THE DIFFERENCE BETWEEN BURNT TOAST AND DIAMOND? (b)

Applying enough pressure
and heat to the ebony
amorphous carbon lazing
upon bread turns donors first
into graphite which helps them
write checks and then makes them pure
tetrahedrons bound to each
other ninety miles under
earth's surface brought towards the crust
by volcanic eruptions
like no shit Black Lives Matter.

Friday, February 5, 2016

A VERY ARTFUL SMEAR

Why accept such a high fee?
That's what they offered, Clinton
offered, clenching cheeks into
a fist. Every posy needs
water, every bee pollen.
Goldman sacks of honey hurt
no one. Heart surgeons and camp
counselors too sought to see her
finger-paint with her middle
fingers, one in de Kooning's
blue bucket, one in the wind.

Saturday, February 6, 2016

CTE (SUPER BOWL 50) CTE

Opposition Research lies
on the couch risking sickness
or suffering the same sneaky
way twenty years of being
hit in the head on the foot-
ball field would. Roger Goodell
said even with sufficient
napkin coverage, enough chips
and guac' while watching debates
could produce chronic trauma-
tic encephalopathy.

for Dave King

duly noted:
http://www.chicagotribune.com/sports/columnists/ct-commissioner-concussions-super-bowl-haugh-spt-0206-20160205-column.html
http://www.chicagotribune.com/sports/football/bears/ct-dave-duerson-roger-goodell-couch-20160207-story.html

Sunday, February 7, 2016

MARCO, *POLO*. MARCO, *POLO*. MARCO …

Man, relieved to know Barack
Obama *knows exactly
what he is doing*. It's looked
that way for a while now, yes.
Thank you for telling us four
times. Was there a hidden ear-
piece turning this sweaty child
in Manchester into the
Manchurian Candidate?
Mainline *this* party: broken
record in an empty suit.

Monday, February 8, 2016

THE SUPREMES

The spirit of liberty
is the spirit which is not
too sure that it is right. Stop
in the name of Learned Hand,
look and listen, as dogma's
freight train blows by, coupling box-
car'd hobos and billionaires.
A certain justice has not
asked a question in ten years
because he already knows—
just so—all the right answers.

Tuesday, February 9, 2016

DIXVILLE NOTCH

In the haunted Balsams Grand
Resort, yawning and vacant
and closed for renovation
like the rest of the country,
nine heroin-plagued zombies
fuss with their midnight makeup
in the freezing fluorescent
bathroom before stalking up
the stairs to cast the very
first votes turning a human
into a granite statue.

Wednesday, February 10, 2016

ANTI-ODE TO CHRIS CHRISTIE

or

BY THE BANKS OF THE GLORIOUS BUT WIDELY TROUBLESOME HUDSON, UNDER THE MORNING'S BLOOD-RED GLOW OF APPROACHING CANNON FIRE, AMIDST THE AGONIZED GROANS OF WOUNDED THOUGH STILL-WILLING VOLUNTEERS, A PASTRAMI SANDWICH LEAPS OFF ITS STEED AND SURRENDERS AT FORT LEE

The Bridge To Nowhere is not
in Alaska but rather
New Jersey. Everything is
legal in New Jersey … 'cept
pumping your own gas and hot
air. Balloon of garrulous
gluttony and self-regard,
this bullied bully flies home
to weigh his campaign's future
only to find he does not
have a scale that counts that low.

for Dean Young

Thursday, February 11, 2016

TO SLEEP, PERCHANCE TO TWEET (FEE-FI-FO-RINA)

She could have been the world's most
powerful woman if just
the world loved her as she loves
herself. Instead, our country's
worst unincarcerated
CEO retreats home to
curl up on her marble slab
corporate board table, to sleep.
In pained dark, her lush iPhone
paints the measured portrait true:
Edward Hopper Twitter feed.

Friday, February 12, 2016

WHEN BLACK HOLES COLLIDE

A chirp! A chirp! David Lynch
robins perched prophetically
on lilac branches could not
produce a more glorious
sound, gravitationally
speaking, than the space-time rip-
ple effect emitted when
a pompous beanbag like Chris
merges, ethics first, with a
sanctimonious broomstick
like Carly. Away they go!

duly noted:
https://www.nytimes.com/2016/02/12/science/ligo-gravitational-waves-black-holes-einstein.html
https://www.pri.org/stories/2016-02-11/listen-collision-two-black-holes-einstein-was-right

Saturday, February 13, 2016

HOME ON THE RANGE: ALEXANDER HAMILTON SINGS "FEDERALIST NO. 68" ON BROADWAY (BADA BING, BADA BOOM)

The process of election affords a moral certainty, that the office of President will never fall to the lot of any man who is not in an eminent degree endowed with the requisite qualifications.
Seldom has *never* been heard as a more discouraging word, regardless of the sky.

duly noted:
http://avalon.law.yale.edu/18th_century/fed68.asp
https://en.wikipedia.org/wiki/Federalist_No._68

Sunday, February 14, 2016

AMY LINDSAY, BE MY VALENTINE

> "I'm a middle-class working
> girl and I had a job to do."
> —Amy Lindsay, on CNN, 2/12/16

Indeed you did. You did it
so well so long in *Perfumed
Garden, Forbidden Sins, Silk
Stalkings, Femalien II, The
Pleasure Zone, Deviant Whores,
Milf* and more Marine Basic
Training Exercises that
at last you "made it" legit,
riding, *Dr. Strangelove*-style,
a Cruz missile attack ad
punking Marco Rubiot.

duly noted:
https://www.nytimes.com/politics/first-draft/2016/02/11/?_r=0
https://en.wikipedia.org/wiki/Amy_Lindsay

Monday, February 15, 2016

SCALIA IN MARFA

There is no good time to die.
But, judicial colossus,
you picked a crummy one. What
was your *intent?* If only,
at your swank hunting ranch, you'd
woken, briefly unholstered
the Second Amendment, rode
into town to see the Judd
boxes in morning's sun, your
take on *textualism*
might have been forever changed.

duly noted:
https://www.washingtonpost.com/news/powerpost/wp/2016/02/13/inside-cibolo-creek-ranch-the-luxury-resort-where-scalia-died
https://chinati.org/collection/donaldjudd

Tuesday, February 16, 2016

GAMECOCKS OF SOUTH CAROLINA

To fight the clucking blue hen
in circled headlights, a good
gamecock must preen, polish, strut
his stuff, walk the walk and talk
the talk about the walk he
walked before he hardly'd learned
to talk, which was his parents'
walk, which comes in handy if
they were poor enough or rich
enough to prove the bloody
point 'bout how damn hard he'll fight.

Wednesday, February 17, 2016

THE LITTLE ARTS: "FEDERALIST NO. 68" CONTINUED

Talents for low intrigue, and the little arts of popularity, may alone suffice to elevate a man to the first honors in a single State; but it will require other talents, and a different kind of merit, to establish him in the esteem and confidence of the whole Union. A dot Ham.

Thursday, February 18, 2016

PROBABILITY THEORY: "FEDERALIST NO. 68" FOR THE LAST TIME

*It will not be too strong to
say, that there will be a con-
stant probability of
seeing the station filled by
characters pre-eminent
for ability and vir-
tue.* Why do you write like you're
running out of lines? A word,
Alexander, from your com-
mander: probability
ain't never constant, ya dig?

Friday, February 19, 2016

DOES A BEAR SHIT IN THE WOODS?

or

WALLS VS. BRIDGES: WHAT'S A META METAPHOR?

Not the screaming Bacon pope
bought by billionaires snorting
culture like blow off Russian
models' boobs, but this Kasich-
safe-for-Terry-Gross-Volvo-
liberals pope, pricking up his
tongue to trash-talk then mic-drop
Trump as *not Christian*. Let's not
spotlight the frenzied millions
force-marched on Church-built gilded
bridges verily to hell.

duly noted:
http://www.cnn.com/2016/02/18/politics/pope-francis-trump-christian-wall/

Saturday, February 20, 2016

1801

Quote: "At the end of his term,
President Adams rushed through
appointments for these judges,
offending Republicans
who thought he should have allowed
the new president to choose."
At Broadway and Wall, shaky
scaffolding surrounds the graves
of Trinity Church, the wind
erasing names. Whenever
we die, we die together.

duly noted:
Ron Chernow, *Alexander Hamilton* (Penguin Books, 2004, p. 647)

Sunday, February 21, 2016

BUSHWHACKING

Dear Jeb! If your brother's sin
was being born on third base
thinking he'd hit a triple,
yours might be that nobody
wants to have a beer with you.
Have your consultants not yet
explained that this heart you show
the margins—immigrants, poor
folks, using a word like *love*
et cetera—is now well past
its sell-by date? It's cold out.

Monday, February 22, 2016

POLYGRAPH

Hell is other people she
knows so well having read some
Sartre in college and gone
on to help the helpless 'stead
of that plush corporate lawyer
gig she brags 'bout turning down.
There was that untidy bit
where she got that rapist off
who'd raped that twelve-year old girl …
laughed 'bout the lie-detector
exonerating her man.

duly noted:
https://www.youtube.com/watch?v=e2f13f2awK4&feature=youtu.be

Tuesday, February 23, 2016

WORKING THE POLLS: SILVER STATE, HEARTS OF GOLD

Other than intelligence,
one of the sexiest things
about them sex-positive
feminists is that they like
sex. Versus them *not-so-much*
feminists. Prostitutes lean
Libertarian: *Pimpin'*
For Paul was working girl group
last two cycles. Now, just read
their lips at Moonlite Bunny
Ranch: *Hookers 4 Hillary*.

duly noted:
https://www.theguardian.com/us-news/2016/feb/15/hookers-for-hillary-clinton-nevada-caucuses-bernie-sanders-moonlite-bunny-ranch

Wednesday, February 24, 2016

MATH (MARCO + TED = DONALD)

One of the Cubans must go.
Cut a deal. Cruz could be Veep.
Cruz could stake out that spare seat
on the Court. The fucking rub:
they loathe each other. One thinks
the other's a rap-loving
RINO. One thinks the other's
a snake so thin you can't force
the math down his throat. Cold War
MAD is what you end up with.
One of the Cubans must go.

duly noted:
RINO: Republican In Name Only
MAD: Mutually Assured Destruction

Thursday, February 25, 2016

PARTY ORGANS

Some folks vote with their heads screwed
on straight, some tilt them to square
with the pain their folks made 'round
the house way back when, when they
learned just how the world hurts. Some
vote with spilled guts, some true hearts,
some spleens spiked with bile and fear.
A sultry movie queen who
feels the Bern just tweeted "I
don't vote with my vagina,"
but tests prove it can be done.

for Barbara Ruhman

duly noted:
https://twitter.com/SusanSarandon/status/699997236500021248

Friday, February 26, 2016

ELEPHANT MEMORIES: THE GRAND OLD PARTY'S PRE-SUPER TUESDAY HOUSTON DEBATE (ALL GUARANTEED VERBATIM)

My father came to this coun-
try with a hundred dollars
in his underwear. My dad
made fifty cents an hour
washing dishes. If Uncle
Joe's smoking like a chimney
everyone is gonna hide
his cigarettes. You know my
father carried mail on his
back. The fruit salad of their
life is what I would look at.

Saturday, February 27, 2016

CULTURE CREATES POLITICS NOT VICE VERSA

or

REPROGRAMMING THE RUBIOT PATRIOT MISSILE DEFENSE SYSTEM

Rubiot is plausible.
He's available. He breathes.
He walks. He memorizes.
He's the wittiest gosh-darned
prettiest of those willing
souls who've not yet abandoned
the mucky race for that huge
white house in the swamp. He lives!
If you feed him the right code
he will, smiling, repeat crude
insults on cue, just like Trump.

Sunday, February 28, 2016

THE IMPACT OF THE BERNIE SANDERS RADIO ADVERTISEMENT BY CURRENT NEW YORK KNICKS FAN & FORMERLY FAMOUS FILMMAKER SPIKE LEE ON THE AFRICAN-AMERICAN VOTERS OF SOUTH CAROLINA, IN REGARDS TO THEIR VOTING IN THE PALMETTO STATE'S FEBRUARY 27, 2016 DEMOCRATIC PRIMARY

Monday, February 29, 2016

CESSATION OF HOSTILITIES

Let's not call it a ceasefire:
Syria, Libya or
Anaheim: Qaddafi or
homegrown guys like William Quigg
or You Know Who: in the end
dragging the dictator out
of the drainpipe he swims in
only to sodomize him
with a bayonet while crowds
jeer is the easy queasy.
Be careful what you wish for.

duly noted:
http://www.nate-thayer.com/kkk-leader-arrested-for-stabbing-protestor-with-u-s-flag-is-trump-supporter/

Tuesday, March 1, 2016

MAKE AMERICA GREAT AGAIN

You could start with slavery.
That would boost profit margins
much more than tax inversions
saving the time and trouble
of stashing your company
abroad. As a free bonus
the slaves would be a future
consuming class after you
freed them, little by little.
Then you could sell them iPhones,
keeping the shackles in place.

Wednesday, March 2, 2016

PINBALL MACHINE

Trump. Trump. Trump. Trump. Trump. Trump. Trump.
Trump Trump. Trump Trump. Trump Trump Trump.
Trump. Trump, Trump. Trump, Trump, Trump. Trump…
Trump Trump Trump. Trump. Trump. Trump. Trump
Trump. Trump, Trump, Trump, Trump. Trump. Trump
Trump Trump. Trump. Trump, Trump. Trump, Trump.
Trump…Trump…Trump…Trump…Trump…Trump…Trump!
Trump Trump. Trump. Trump, Trump, Trump. Trump.
Trump? Trump. Trump? Trump. Trump? Trump Trump.
Trump. Trump. Trump. Trump? Trump! Trump!! Trump!!!
Trump Trump Trump Trump Trump Trump Trump.

duly noted:
http://www.realclearpolitics.com/articles/2016/02/29/justice_thomas_asks_question_in_court_1st_time_in_ten_years_129819.html
see February 8, 2016, "THE SUPREMES"

Thursday, March 3, 2016

THE BODY OF QADDAFI

displayed in a freezer lay
for days after his death so
the public would really know
he was dead. The nice walk-in
industrial freezer held
his son Mutassim too. Some
drove hundreds of miles cross
country to see proof he'd died.
One such man, so driven, said:
"God made the pharaoh as an
example to the others."

Friday, March 4, 2016

CULTURE OF COMPLAINT
(DONALD'S VICTIMIZATION DEPARTMENT)

These people in Washington
are horribly hurting US.
They are so so stupid but
smart enough to rule us wrong.
Mean/while leaders of China,
Iran, Japan, Mexico
and Vietnam eat our lunch,
glaring and laughing at us,
even as we stand in line
at food trucks waiting to eat
the lunch they made us so good.

Saturday, March 5, 2016

FEBRUARY 2, 2012
(BUT SUCCESSFUL NONETHELESS: SUFFICIENTLY SUCCESSFUL TO UNDERSTAND WHAT IT TAKES TO GET AMERICA TO BE THE MOST ATTRACTIVE PLACE IN THE WORLD FOR INNOVATORS, ENTREPRENEURS, AND JOB CREATORS)

*There are some things that you just
can't imagine happening
in your life. This is one of
them: being in Donald Trump's
magnificent hotel and
having his endorsement is
a delight. I'm so honored
and pleased to have his endorse-
ment. I've spent my life in the
private sector, not quite as
successful as this guy but …*

duly noted:
https://www.youtube.com/watch?v=nmwzGMmGcJw

Sunday, March 6, 2016

THINGS DONALD TRUMP WOULD LIKE TO STRAP TO THE ROOF OF HIS CAR FOR VACATION-DRIVING PURPOSES

Little Marco in a dog
cage. Mitt Romney's stained copy
of the *Book of Mormon*. A
pallet of Marla Maples'
panties. Barack Obama's
Kenyan birth certificate
in a laminate necklace
wind-blown around the stout neck
of Ted Cruz, Isadora
Duncanish, the sweet weeping
willow branch fast approaching.

for Gail Collins

Monday, March 7, 2016

FRACTIONAL INTEREST

Like Alan Keyes and Herman
Cain before him, Ben Carson
left the operating room
(stage right) without having served
a sole Oval Office day.
Sadly undone: repealing
Black History Month, or at least
shortnin' it from the shortest
month of the year to three-fifths
of that month, in keeping with
our Founding Fathers' intent.

Tuesday, March 8, 2016

REALTY FEALTY MEETS GOEBBELS GOBBLEDYGOOK

or

THE PLEDGE

Always felt creepy at school.
Saying one nation, under
God, caused cooties plus confused
grin. To be part of something
bigger than your skin appeals
to the scared child in every
adult: *That I, no matter*
how I feel, no matter what
the conditions, if there's a
hurricane or whatever …
will vote for _____.
              Fill in the blank

duly noted:
http://www.cbsnews.com/news/trump-led-salute-at-florida-rally-raises-evocative-concerns-on-social-media/

Wednesday, March 9, 2016

HEALTH INSURANCE (REMOVING THE LINES AROUND THE STATES)

Michigan was caught screwing
around with Mississippi
in the back of Britney Spears'
pickup. Robert Johnson and
William Faulkner approved, sang
'bout it, but did not other-
wise participate. Then, last
night, while the East Coast gently
slept, gushy fresh Hawaii
accepted the most pointed
advances of Idaho.

Thursday, March 10, 2016

ON THE QUESTION OF BERNIE'S JUDAISM

If my menschy right-wing-scare-
monger-please-God-rest-his-soul-
grandfather arose from his
grave like that other wise guy
with the long locks blue eyes beard
in most pictures and chill words
about turned cheeks and fishes
he would find himself in a
classic Talmudic-wrestling-
chokehold-takedown-grudge-Drudge-death-
match asking: Jew or no Jew?

Friday, March 11, 2016

THE TWELTH DEBATE
(MIAMI SOUND MACHINE)

Little baby cockapoos,
nipping at his trouser cuffs,
chase each other's tales across
the warm, fuzzy stage, a con-
test to pick a pedigreed
mutt from the shrunken litter.
While Texas argues purebred,
juicy red stakes on the floor
go shockingly uneaten.
The piano has been drinking
and the bar stools are on fire.

Saturday, March 12, 2016

THE BRIDGE AND TUNNEL CROWD

Remember when amnesty
was a good word? The fragrance
of forgiveness infusing
every Vietnam War draft
dodger's overdue dinner
back home. Now the talk of walls
is tall and spurs rip ripe flesh
of whatever horse brought you.
Smashed glass of freedom, a toast
for this sad ballad country
that orphans its immigrants.

for Lin-Manuel Miranda

Sunday, March 13, 2016

BLUE CITIZENS UNITED

Priorities USA.
Generation Forward. Planned
Parenthood Votes. Women Vote.
TuckFrump.com. National
Nurses United. Make A-
merica Awesome. Black Lives
Matter. American Bridge
21st Century. Blue
South. Billionaires For Bernie.
Draft Biden. NextGen Climate
Action. Ready For Warren.

duly noted (via OpenSecrets.org):
Priorities USA supports Clinton; *Generation Forward* supported O'Malley; *Planned Parenthood Votes* supports Clinton; *Women Vote* supports Clinton; TuckFrump.com opposes Trump; *National Nurses United* supports Sanders; *Make America Awesome* opposes Trump; *Black Lives Matter* supports ?; *American Bridge 21st Century* supports ?; *Blue South* supports ?; *Billionaires For Bernie* supports Sanders; *Draft Biden* supported Biden; *NextGen Climate Action* supports ?; *Ready For Warren* supports Warren.

Monday, March 14, 2016

REPORTS OF SLIGHT DUST-UPS AT RALLIES FOR THE DONALD IN THE WAKE OF SAINT NANCY'S SAD PASSING, LONG-PREDICTED BY HER ASTUTE ASTROLOGER

Used to have real politics
where if you didn't like his
drift maybe your fist would touch
his nose hey no big deal then
a beer a shot a bandage.
"Politically correct"
has queered it all starting with
your queers your welfare queens your
strapping young bucks Reagan put
it right like we forgot how
this fucking country got made.

Tuesday, March 15, 2016

THE IDES OF MARCH:
JOHN WILKES BOOTH, GEORGE CLOONEY,
AND TWENTY-THREE VOTES OF THE KNIFE

Any old scapegoat won't do.
To wash away our sins we
need a truly buff mountain
goat. Enter the haruspex
Spurinna: *Aye, Caesar, but
not gone.* There's your money shot.
Let's settle debts. Empire or
Republic? Senator or
Guv'nor? History or fiction?
My friend you might find the wind
is blowin' in the answer.

Wednesday, March 16, 2016

INSULAR AREA CNMI
(AREA CODE 670)

or

THE MARIANAS
(ISLANDS OF THE THIEVES)

No man is an island I
sang at camp but no island
is an island Organic
Acts assure. Galleons come and
go, talking of Magellan.
With no private property,
natives "stole" a skiff roped to
the poop of the captain's ship.
The *Enola Gay* takes off,
this time with nine delegates
in the businessman's bomb bay.

duly noted:
http://thehill.com/blogs/ballot-box/273017-trump-wins-northern-mariana-islands-caucus

Thursday, March 17, 2016

ELEPHANT EARS & NEVERGLADES:
MARCO'S MEMOIR

Always said his parents fled
Castro's Cuba until oops
papers showed they appeared in
Florida years sooner: Fidel
was still cooling his cigar
in Mexico. If only
the lie'd been bigger he could
have gone farther. This *climate*.
If you hold his right ear up
to your ear, you can hear the
rising ocean wave goodbye.

Friday, March 18, 2016

PROMISE RIOT

Though long-predicted the scene
is still one of shock and dis-
belief as you see clearly
now promises are breaking
out all over the vast floor
of this convention and we
have new footage for you where
you can see Security
try but fail to stop a lie
from just sucker-punching a
rumor on the street outside.

Saturday, March 19, 2016

BRACKET BUSTING (MARCH MADNESS)

The experts have their rankings
swipe screens clickers data sets
mined for historical truths
we hold not self-evident.
A fifteenth seed tenderly
planted in someone's loamy
imagination may spring
entrepreneurial, whole,
while the first fourteen find no
purchase. Across the country:
a regression to the mean.

for Adam "Red Dog" Blitz

Sunday, March 20, 2016

SPELLING BEE (C, D, F)

What you tried to do ain't what
you did. Mathematical
proofs argue (elegantly)
this tunneling mole into
your intentions as far back
as junior high. In the gym,
crepe bunting and wobbly booths
spell out the phat chance your vote
might, against published odds, make
the difference between raising
and razing Arizona.

for Sam Ekwurtzel

Monday, March 21, 2016

PLANS FOR ALTERING THE DESERT: SONORAN BORDER WALL

After the candidates leave,
in spring night-blooming cacti
will wave white power flower
flags of surrender. Honey
bees, lesser long-nosed bats, black-
chinned hummingbirds, white-winged doves,
gilded flickers and Gila
'peckers all know money is
the pollen of politics.
A wall built out of wooden
ribs of shot dead saguaros.

Tuesday, March 22, 2016

BEING / RESPONSIBLE

To move underground freely
is a miracle: engine
of progress, the spinning minds
of engineered machines tuned
to what we want. Another
wonder: to fly from Brussels
to any spot on the globe
without wings, just the ticket.
What hunger prowls in human
beings who bomb, who fight to
claim responsibility?

duly noted:
http://www.bbc.com/news/world-europe-35869254

Wednesday, March 23, 2016

Q: WHY DO PEOPLE TAKE SUCH AN
     INSTANT DISLIKE TO TED CRUZ?
A: IT SAVES TIME

He leads with his chin only
because it was bolted on
by Carpentry while Makeup
was on union-mandated
break. His sphincter grimace melts
into a shit-eating smile
when he's self-satisfied, like
'bout always. His sad puppy
eyes turn Doberman upon
swift attack. His eyebrows arch:
arch silent movie villain.

Thursday, March 24, 2016

COUNTING THE DEAD

Counting casualties like wired
crows: all the same, all different.
Bloody bits nail-blown onto
baggage scales preserved now for
DNA discovery.
When we count victims do we
count the suicide bombers?
They belong but don't belong.
They are, were, people. Oh Lord
are they not in that number
when the saints go marching in?

Friday, March 25, 2016

TRUMP CARD SLASH ACE IN THE HOLE

or

HOW COULD THERE BE FIVE WOMEN ON THE PLANET WHO WOULD EVEN *WANT* TO HAVE *EXTRA EXTRA READ ALL ABOUT IT* EXTRA-MARITAL SEX WITH TED CRUZ?

Why does the "Lyin' Ted" meme
have legs? *Katrina Pierson*
works for him. Last night she turned
her Instagram private. *Am-
anda Carpenter* stonewalls
on TV. *Sarah Isgur
Flores* must be why a Ted
super PAC strangely gave huge
bucks to a Carly super
PAC. FEC is interesTED.
TrusTED just might be busTED.

Saturday, March 26, 2016

NOT EXACTLY LINCOLN VS. DOUGLAS

After mating does Ted Cruz
get eaten by the female
wolf spider? Obviously
not, or he would not breathe to
spit these words yesterday: *He's
a man for whom a term was
coined for copulating with
a rodent. Well, let me be
clear: Donald Trump may be a
rat, but I have no desire
to copulate with him.* True?

duly noted:
http://www.esquire.com/news-politics/news/a43332/ted-cruz-donald-trump-rat-copulate/

Sunday, March 27, 2016

1ST QUARTER 2016, DRAWN AND QUARTERED

Asadabad, Istanbul,
Zliten, Quetta, Kouyape,
Ouagadougou, Bodo, Zhob,
Mogadishu, Kerawa,
Kidal, Dalori, Dikwa,
Baidoa, Ntombi, Homs,
Meme, Grand-Bassam, Gombi,
Maiduguri, Yakshari,
Charsadda, Muqdadiyah,
Ankara, Brussels, Aden,
Iskandariya, Lahore …

Monday, March 28, 2016

THE BLACKER THE BERRY, THE SWEETER THE JUICE (a)

Stud soldier turned CIA
head David Petraeus mis-
handled his mistress as she
lapped Top Secret stuff off his
laptop while writing *All In*.
Now having a Paula Broad-
well problem's not Hillary's
classified problem, but she
sports the same lawyer, David
Kendall, who will vet what her
mistresses may have consumed.

THE BLACKER THE BERRY, THE SWEETER THE JUICE   (b)

James Clapper, David Pecker:
names too phony for fiction.
Whether Hillary is gay
or straight, who cares? as she may
be bi- or even a- *at*
this juncture, the elder Bush
would say. Fine. But for Huma
Abedin to marry that
sexting Weiner guy is some
kind of Texas hold 'em tell.
What card might the server serve?

THE BLACKER THE BERRY, THE SWEETER THE JUICE (c)

Cheryl Mills founded the Black-Ivy Group. Michelle Bachman said the Muslim Brotherhood had made "deep penetration" in our soft center. Sydney Leathers crashed Carlos Danger's party. Roger Stone (leaving no rock unturned nor rat unfucked) states Just Sue If Untrue. Someday, Ted will give a TED Talk: *Cuban Mistress Crisis*.

duly noted:
http://starcasm.net/archives/234348
Sydney Leathers "Hero's Trending" August 2012: 1. President Obama 2. Bill Maher 3. Anthony Weiner 4. Bernie Sanders 5. Julian Assange 6. Keith Olbermann 7. Alan Grayson 8. Rachel Maddow 9. Jon Stewart 10. Charlie Sheen

Tuesday, March 29, 2016

FORMULA (PARTY OF LINCOLN)

A sun forever setting.
Bitter wrongs, father to son.
An unkindness of money.
Aroma of indifference.
Mother's milk, poisoned, add death.
White snakeroot, coffin pegs, cold.
Meals of sweaty food and noise.
Slashed for reading, books destroyed.
Whipped, beaten, undefeated.
Vaulting ambition, geared heat.
Cardinal in late spring snow.

Wednesday, March 30, 2016

MANHANDLING

What's simple about simple
battery? What's casual
about casualties? If if
a man holds a woman's arm:
crime. This fragile flower thing
smells unbecoming. Women
fought to be in the scrum now
what have we become? Double
AAs holding, losing, filing
charges, depleting ourselves,
juiceless in/on Jupiter.

duly noted:

Florida state statute 784.03(1)(a): "The offense of battery occurs when a person: 1. Actually and intentionally touches or strikes another person against the will of the other; or 2. Intentially causes bodily harm to another person."

http://www.politico.com/story/2016/03/trump-campaign-manager-charged-with-misdemeanor-battery-221336

Thursday, March 31, 2016

SPIN ROOM: DISTAFF DIVISION

The uterus as focal
point. Discuss! Each candidate
claims special relation, plus
appeal to other party
organs: brain, heart, liver, lungs
the odds-on favorites. Favorite
sons' and daughters' taut clawing
for the tractive pull of polls.
Vexing and vague unconquered
territory, the body
has always been politic.

Friday, April 1, 2016

ONLY BECAUSE THROWING SOMEONE UNDER THE PLANE IS AN ART WHICH HAS YET TO BE PERFECTED, OR EVEN POPULARIZED, AND IS NOT YET TRENDING

Back in the day you only
had to talk. Reporters would
report. Now you have to *walk
back* what you talked if you talked
wrong. That walk is more exhaust-
ing than a thousand tweets. You
have to throw people *under
the bus* who deserve it or
you will appear overly
loyal and/or weak. If you
have no bus, you must rent one.

Saturday, April 2, 2016

METHINKS THE CANDIDATE DOTH
EVIDENCE A FEARSOME LACK OF LOGIC
FOR ONE WHO WAS ONCE A STEADFAST
& DOUGHTY MEMBER OF THE MUCH-
LAUDED DEBATING ASSOCIATION OF THAT
VENERABLE, IVY-BEDECKED INSTITUTION
OF HIGHER LEARNING, PRINCETON, FROM
WHERE HE SPRANG SO STARCHED & SPRY

or

CRINGE

You try to raise your kids right
but if my rough-and-tumble
teenage son raped my virgin
teenage daughter (let's hope it
would be rape or things would be
even much worser) Ted Cruz
insists my girl bring any
resulting miracle to
term or she'd be murderer …
but insists equally he
does not want women punished.

Sunday, April 3, 2016

TED CRUZ PONDERS "THOSE 55 MILLION SOULS" LOST TO ABORTION SINCE ROE V. WADE: "WE CANNOT KNOW HOW MANY INVENTORS, MUSICIANS, SCIENTISTS, ATHLETES, PHYSICIANS, AND ENTREPRENEURS WERE NEVER ALLOWED TO BREATHE THEIR FIRST BREATH OF LIFE"

Forget the guitarist more
blazing than Hendrix, the jump-
shooter purer than Curry.
How many job-creating
baby entrepreneurs went
unborn? On his first day home
he could have schemed the Uber
for mothers' milk, TaskRabbit
for his diapers. Roe Roe Roe
your boat gently up the stream
of royalties and sushi.

Monday, April 4, 2016

ON OBSERVING THE STRANGE NATURALLY-OCCURRING OR PERHAPS MAN-MADE PHENOMENON WHEREBY DEBATE MODERATORS, TOWN HALL ATTENDEES, NEWS ANCHORS, AND BEAT REPORTERS HAVE STOPPED EVEN ASKING THE REPUBLICAN CANDIDATES ABOUT CLIMATE CHANGE

It would be almost funny—
Beckett or Mamet funny,
tangled Shakespeare funny—if
the action of the present
upon the future were not
plain depredation. Act Twelve.
Curtain. We are not even
rearranging deck chairs on
the *Titanic* anymore.
We are just waiting to see
which deck chairs will get wet last.

for Spencer Glendon

Tuesday, April 5, 2016

ON, WISCONSIN!

Leave the cows alone. They're fed
up with photo ops, cheesehead
jokes, pols acting rural while
briefcased, power-tied sluts ear-
piece orders from the black bench
seats of idling Suburbans
and Navigators. Secret
Service sunglasses throw back
the puffy passing clouds kids
draw. Let's pretend they moo too:
Can we give our milk in peace?

Wednesday, April 6, 2016

THE ACTION

Betting-markets quiver, keen.
Probabilities skinny.
She bruises. Coughs. She sputters.
The punishing sun spreads hate.
First dates, pajamas, planes, sleep.
Bark, bark, bark, bark. Meow clock.
Time is the matter at hand.
Outrage pours from the plugged tap.
Lipstick on pigs: attractive.
Like and dislike, like dislike.
A stone in every worn shoe.

Thursday, April 7, 2016

QUALIFICATIONS: RACE RIOT

Money be the mother's milk
of politics, so a fresh
forty-four mill in Sanders'
bottle allows crying rights
re: robber barons and free
tuition till Fresno in
June. Chicken in every pot,
pot in every kitchen, meth
fumes rising from every well-
armed park. Napalm-hot, just like
'68. Bern, Baby, Bern!

Friday, April 8, 2016

LIKE WATCHING YOUR HAIRY-EARED GRANDFATHER GO TOO FAR ON THE DANCE FLOOR AT A BAR MITZVAH WITH A WOMAN NOT HIS WIFE, YOU JUST WISH HE WOULDN'T

Her email smells off. Hawkish
on Iraq when she shoulda
woulda coulda known better.
Imperial Clintonish
entitlement, duh. Too much
testosterone? Look under
her hood; hard cash from oily,
gassy and banky interests.
The problematic pantsuits,
the clanging dull stump speeches.
But she's not not qualified.

duly noted:
https://www.youtube.com/watch?v=DPAbk9ofjOo

Saturday, April 9, 2016

IT'S A WONDERFUL LIFE

In Bern's dream, Bailey Brothers
Building and Loan has grown strong
with the savings of average
Americans. The glow of
Christmas and Hanukkah (and
Kwanzaa) lights illuminates
a poster for the student
loan-forgiveness pogrom in
the gay window. Outside, snow
falls, warmly. Henry Potter:
in jail. "The End" is the start.

for Rob Usdan

Sunday, April 10, 2016

ROY COHN

Goes to figure Trump was taught
the razor-bladed ropes by
a homophobic homo-
sexual, Jew-hating Jew
who never met a kike he
liked. Julius, Ethel. Pow-
er! *All I can tell you is
he's been vicious to others
in his protection of me.*
Never mistake Gene for Joe
McCarthy. Past is present.

for Louis Schump

duly noted:
http://www.politico.com/magazine/story/2016/04/donald-trump-roy-cohn-mentor-joseph-mccarthy-213799

Monday, April 11, 2016

FADE IN:

EXT. "SECOND BAPTIST HIGH SCHOOL" (HOUSTON, 1988) – ESTABLISHING – DAY

A teenage boy appears on bicycle, in checked shirt, in front of a fountain.

      TED
Aspirations? Is that like sweat on my butt? No, no, I see: what I want to do in life…? My aspiration is to be in a teen tit film like that guy in … *Malibu Bikini Beach Shop*. Well, other than that, uh, take over the world. World domination. You know, rule everything. Rich. Powerful. That sort of stuff.

duly noted:
http://talkingpointsmemo.com/livewire/teen-ted-cruz-world-domination

Tuesday, April 12, 2016

MISSIONARIES! MISSIONARIES! WE'RE ON TOP!!!

or

THE LAWN SIGNS TALLY BERNIE 7,
EVERYBODY ELSE 2

Walla Walla, Washington,
killed its Indians in due
course of human events, so
laying the path for the wine
tastings and Main Street Guitar
Festivals of present-day
Postmodernia. Whitman
profs amble about, disgraced—
teams still the Missionaries.
Votes for alternatives pour
in. Enter Reverse Cowgirls.

Wednesday, April 13, 2016

LEWIS & CLARK

All schools badge-buff famous grads,
erasing problem offspring
Stalinstyle. Who's kidding whom?
On campus tour, her face pokes
out from behind the Bernie-
postered dorm window. Grizzly
memory so rank in still graves
they itch to cock their blunder-
busses and finger triggers,
as they have a special one
in Monica Lewinsky.

Thursday, April 14, 2016

SHELL COMPANY

Double-Irish arrangement.
Front company. Hold Co. New
Co. Dummy. Special Purpose
Vehicle. Shadow banking.
LLCs, LPs, offshore
trusts, liquidity and grease.
Avoidance evasion. Babes
in Toyland, Toys in Babeland.
Ahhh! Whisper-quiet stirring
rabbits ooze juice: all campaigns
have some pump and dump to them.

Friday, April 15, 2016

DABIQ MARKS MUSLIM REPRESENTATIVE KEITH ELLISON (D-MINN.) AND CLOSE CLINTON CONFIDANTE HUMA ABEDIN, ALSO MUSLIM, FOR DEATH, AS APOSTATES AND OVERT CRUSADERS NOT EVEN WEARING CLOAK OF *DA'WAH* WHILE ENFORCING LAWS OF *KUFR* (THEY COULD GO ON)

When Republican super
PACs mark you for death, they mean
it metaphorically. Though
to be real, Republicans
are not, by nature, meta-
phoric. Genetically I
mean. ISIS, ISIL, Daesh—call
them what you will or what they
call their lying, torturing,
raping, murdering selves—they
are less metaphoric still.

duly noted:
http://www.upi.com/Top_News/US/2016/04/13/Clinton-aide-Minnesota-rep-on-list-marked-for-death-in-militant-magazine/7371460583992/
https://en.wikipedia.org/wiki/Dabiq_(magazine)

Thursday, April 14, 2016

SHELL COMPANY

Double-Irish arrangement.
Front company. Hold Co. New
Co. Dummy. Special Purpose
Vehicle. Shadow banking.
LLCs, LPs, offshore
trusts, liquidity and grease.
Avoidance evasion. Babes
in Toyland, Toys in Babeland.
Ahhh! Whisper-quiet stirring
rabbits ooze juice: all campaigns
have some pump and dump to them.

Friday, April 15, 2016

DABIQ MARKS MUSLIM REPRESENTATIVE KEITH ELLISON (D-MINN.) AND CLOSE CLINTON CONFIDANTE HUMA ABEDIN, ALSO MUSLIM, FOR DEATH, AS APOSTATES AND OVERT CRUSADERS NOT EVEN WEARING CLOAK OF *DA'WAH* WHILE ENFORCING LAWS OF *KUFR* (THEY COULD GO ON)

When Republican super
PACs mark you for death, they mean
it metaphorically. Though
to be real, Republicans
are not, by nature, meta-
phoric. Genetically I
mean. ISIS, ISIL, Daesh—call
them what you will or what they
call their lying, torturing,
raping, murdering selves—they
are less metaphoric still.

duly noted:
http://www.upi.com/Top_News/US/2016/04/13/Clinton-aide-Minnesota-rep-on-list-marked-for-death-in-militant-magazine/7371460583992/
https://en.wikipedia.org/wiki/Dabiq_(magazine)

Saturday, April 16, 2016

A MORAL ECONOMY OF MOMENTS: BEFORE JETTING OFF FOR LESBOS, TIME FOR A BAGEL WITH A PAPAL SCHMEAR

Pope: *We have created new idols. The worship of the golden calf of old has found a new and heartless image in the cult of money and the dictatorship of an economy which is faceless and lacking any truly humane goal.* Music to Bernie's ears! Turn that papal amp to fuckin' eleven!

duly noted:
https://www.bloomberg.com/politics/articles/2016-04-15/sanders-steps-away-from-new-york-campaign-for-vatican-conference

Sunday, April 17, 2016

SUNDAY SERMON:
AVOIDING THE SLIPPERY SLOPE (FROM THE
USE OF OBSCENE DEVICES TO ENGAGING IN
CONSENSUAL ADULT INCEST OR BIGAMY)

or

TED CRUZ, 2007:
SOLICITOR GENERAL / TEXAS RANGER

*There is no substantive-due-
process right to stimulate
one's genitals for non-med-
ical purposes unre-
lated to procreation
or outside of an inter-
personal relationship.
The Texas Penal Code pro-
hibits the advertisement
and sale of dildos, arti-
ficial vaginas, and oth-*

duly noted:

All *italicized* language lifted from the Solictor General's legal brief arguing the State's defense of Sections 43.21 and 43.23 of the Texas Penal Code, known as the "Obscene Device Law," in the case "Reliable Consultants v. Abbott," and thereafter inserted into the above. The state further argued that it had "police-power interests in protecting public morals" and that "any alleged right associated with obscene devices" is not "deeply rooted in the Nation's history and traditions." The basic thrust of the State's position was in "discouraging prurient interests in autonomous sex and the pursuit of sexual gratification unrelated to procreation."

Monday, April 18, 2016

CARPETBAGGING / CARPET BOMBING

or

THE B-52'S ARE NOT A FUNNY BAND

If only they'd loved you more
or better, you'd be less apt
to need the widespread rapture.
Project *Sun Bath* paved the way:
*Operation Arc Light, Op-
eration Rolling Thunder*
made the Theater glow. Then, "Big
Belly" modifications
upped *Linebacker II*'s payload.
Obliteration might mean
the love comes later, afresh.

for Julian Lage

duly noted:
Sir Arthur Tedder, May 6, 1943, during The Tunisia Campaign, noted in the press as "Tedder's bomb-carpet" or "Tedder's carpet."

Tuesday, April 19, 2016

7-ELEVEN

All things are about themselves.
When a candidate needs to
evoke the heroic trope
regarding firefighters
and police saving citi-
zens empirically from crum-
bling towers, but instead sub-
consciously invokes Slurpees,
Wild Cherry Slurpee Donuts,
fat-sizzling dogs and nitrate-
charged jerky, we know we're home.

duly noted:
http://nypost.com/2016/04/19/donald-trump-confuses-911-with-7-eleven/

Wednesday, April 20, 2016

FIGURES OF SPEECH

What does Schenectady stand
for? Might tight Kasich excrete
a delegate there, his first
since tuba-fart Ohio?
Big whoop! Synecdoche trumps
metonymy. Sinatra
sailing over riddling strings
favored asyndeton, and
he could make it anywhere,
including in this ballroom
amid dim echoism.

for W. S. Di Piero

Thursday, April 21, 2016

GUESS WHO?

Outsider. No Big Money
donors. Against Iraq War.
Won't let folks die in the streets—
everyone covered. Appeals
to angry "disenfranchised"
whites. Voodoo economics.
Tells it like it is. Against
Free Trade. Against rigged system.
All enemies corrupt pols.
Woodpecker stump speech. Base: low-
info, rabid, *believers*.

Friday, April 22, 2016

PRINCE: I WANNA BE YOUR LOVER
CRUZ: HAVE WE GONE STARK-RAVING NUTS?

Imagine Ted as Tom Jones
singing "Kiss." Imagine him
doing "The Bird" with Morris
Day & The Time. Pop-locking
with Chaka Khan through "I Feel
For You." Full-face like Sinead
lipsyncing "Nothing Compares
2 U." Complaining about
his "Manic Monday" workload
with The Bangles. No? Prince would,
laughing, like right now, and still.

for Prince Rogers Nelson, in memoriam
(June 7, 1958–April 21, 2016)

duly noted:
Cruz: http://therightscoop.com/ted-cruz-slams-trump-on-transgender-bathroom-position-have-we-gone-stark-raving-nuts/
Prince: https://www.youtube.com/watch?v=FwWBJ3U3THs

Saturday, April 23, 2016

GUESS WHO? TOO

Raise taxes on the rich! Check.
Not religious. Check. (Though *kvells*
over unhidden Jewish
family.) Uncheckable math
on bold proposals. Check. Scant
record of accomplishments.
Check. Gun rights advocate. Check.
Repeats himself. Repeats him-
self. Check. Check. LGBT
okay! Check. Bathroom bills: thumbs
down. Check. Few black votes. Checkmate.

Sunday, April 24, 2016

PENNSYLVANIA LOOPHOLE PRIMARY

Before loophole meant a means
of escape or evasion,
or opportunity to
elude a rule or law, it
meant a smallish or narrow
opening in a wall, for
looking through, for admitting
light and air, but mostly in
a fortification, for
discharging missiles against
a sworn enemy outside.

Monday, April 25, 2016

TAG TEAM

Being *mathematically
dead* has its advantages:
freedom to draw and paint out-
side the explicit boxes
pre-printed on stern white sheets.
Ted, meet John. John, Ted. Agreed!
Pro wrestling ain't phony. Just
the results are phony. That's
why it's called *professional*.
The feelings of the paying
customers always be real.

for Sam Seaman

Tuesday, April 26, 2016

ACELA PRIMARY PROGNOSTICATION

The writing is on the wall
so I read what it said: *TUCK
FRUMP.* Buddy, the just-dead ex-
Rhody boss, stuffs a body
in his Caddy trunk, gestures
with lit cigarette, and drives
playing "The Summer Wind" down
to the deserted river.
Splash! The big difference between
big and small time can be just
Chris Paul's third metacarpal.

for Mark Rowland

Wednesday, April 27, 2016

GOP CARTOON

So the snarly Tea Party
prig and the pockmarked pancake-
into-piehole fracking free-
loader get swirled up into
a dark stormtrooper sky by
The Tangerine Tornado
then fall to the street where they
get turned two-dimensional
by a steamroller. The whole
Party has poopy diapers.
Now who's going to change them?

Thursday, April 28, 2016

LOVE MATCH

In search of a running mate
with the right plumbing, Ted Cruz
fingers a female mammal
with the look of a police
artist's facial composite
who sings to his dainty girls:
Don't enter the wrong restrooms
where transgender "men" ride brooms!
Is this the first time a rat
has ever climbed aboard a
sinking ship for just deserts?

duly noted:
http://thehill.com/blogs/ballot-box/presidential-races/277921-fiorina-sings-at-vp-announcement
http://uproxx.com/tv/the-daily-show-carly-fiorina-singing/

Friday, April 29, 2016

JUST AS PEARL SKIRVIN BECAME PERLE MESTA, CARA CARLETON SNEED BECAME CARLY FIORINA

Carly's creepy *We get to
play on the bus all day* song
for Caroline and Catherine
Cruz is to the tune of I.
Berlin's "You're Just in Love" from
an obscure Ethel Merman
musical, *Call Me Madam*,
a political satire
based on the real-life doings
of a D.C. socialite,
"The Hostess With The Mostest."

duly noted:
https://www.youtube.com/watch?v=2LAijDQ2cIE
http://content.time.com/time/covers/0,16641,19490314,00.html
Richard Nixon, Grand Jury Testimony, June 1975: "Perle Mesta wasn't sent to Luxembourg because she had big bosoms. Perle Mesta went to Luxembourg because she made a good contribution."

Saturday, April 30, 2016

MONEY

When she wins big she gets all
munificent, for a mo-
ment, baking-tin voice warming
to the occasion as she
friskily cuddles her hurt-
ing opponent. She mouths: *I
applaud Senator Sanders
for challenging us to get
unaccountable money
out of our politics.* She
meant uncountable money.

for Brad Swift

Sunday, May 1, 2016

MISSING THINGS

A carpet without bombing.
Clinton's Goldman Sachs shining
speech transcripts. Donald's tax re-
turns. Carly's heebie-jeebie
ditty: The Last Three Verses.
Babies being offered up
by parents to be kissed on
the campaign trail. (No one wants
these guys leaving bodily
fluids on their babies.) The
H in huge. Huckabee. Jeb!

Monday, May 2, 2016

WORDS OF THE DAY

Amid friction of frantic
birling, *all wet* tumescent
bromides and jejune blarney
pockmark wayworn galumphing.
Slugabed pundits tsk tsk
obstreperous parvenus.
Haplography gives us rump.
Minimax gives us flummoxed
melees splotched by tommyrot.
Perhaps we will end with one
big fat kakistocracy.

Tuesday, May 3, 2016

YOU ARE SURROUNDED, GIVE YOURSELF UP (A NEW SONG FOR TED'S BUS)

Indiana wants me, Lord
I can't go back there. If a
man ever needed dyin',
he did. No one had the right
to say what he said about
you. And it's so cold and lone-
ly here without you. Out there
the law's a comin', I'm scared
and so tired of runnin'. It
hurts to see the man that I've
become. (Etc.) (Sirens.)

duly noted:
https://www.youtube.com/watch?v=KNM5g2ARGyY
http://www.songfacts.com/detail.php?id=3392
http://www.amiright.com/misheard/song/indianawantsme.shtml

Wednesday, May 4, 2016

DEARLY DEPAR*TED*

In Ted's household—he took pains
to inform us—when a child
behaves in a childish way,
he (meaning she) gets spanked. *That*
will teach them to hate (and love)
strongmen. Not strong men. You just
got taken to the woodshed
and whupped. Ass ripped up. Beaten
with a switch. Belted. Hoosier
daddy now? Ohhh-bliv-i-on.
Have you learned your lesson, boy?

Thursday, May 5, 2016

ONE IS THE LONELIEST NUMBER

Trouble remembering that
Howard Dean Steve Forbes and Newt
Gingrich each won two states Ed
Muskie won three to five based
how you count Pats Buchanan
and Robertson both won four
and Linda Ronstadt shagmate
Jerry Brown won six last time
he ran means you won't recall
squat about sad sack Kasich
some years hence since he won one

Friday, May 6, 2016

START ME UP

Mick: I went to London School
of Economics. Donald:
I went to Wharton, one of
the best, the best school really.
Mick: "Brown Sugar" at rallies?
Y'know what that song's about?
Donald: Heroin? Slavery?
Sex? I'm cool with those last two
plus we both know it's not words
it's the *feeling* we're selling.
Mick: You make a grown man cry.

duly noted:
http://www.nbcnews.com/pop-culture/music/rolling-stones-tell-donald-trump-stop-playing-their-music-rallies-n568581
http://www.thedailybeast.com/articles/2016/02/10/rolling-stones-say-trump-never-asked-to-use-their-songs.html

Saturday, May 7, 2016

MOUNTEBANK

Charlatan, huckster, grifter,
fraud: the riches of English
teem with phony gold: sham, quack,
fake, cheat, con. But one term rules,
king for our malevolent
escalator descender
who firmly mounts the public
bench as a loyal German
shepherd mounts a quivering mutt:
by instinct, without a care,
and with a glint in his eye.

for Norman Atkins

Sunday, May 8, 2016

MOTHER'S DAY

In the wee village of Tong,
just up from Stornoway on
the wild Isle of Lewis,
was Mary Anne MacLeod born,
10th of May, Nineteen and Twelve,
in No. 3 Tong, a croft
house made of peat smoke, porridge
and potatoes, flaying thatch
of Gaelic hymn and some trout.
Years later her son would sport
her Viking helmet of hair.

for Lucy Skaer

Monday, May 9, 2016

APP

Donald has an app to make
the powerless feel power
full: it imagines you watch-
ing him tweet pics of the tits
of his wife bathed in the gilt
of his name riding the Fear
Float of convenient scapegoats
parading from his fishy
lips. Women's version: to come.
The app is free (of course) but
you will pay a special price.

Tuesday, May 10, 2016

BETTER APP

Bernie has an app to make
the powerless feel power-
ful: it imagines you beat-
ing a banker or broker
on The Street with a hemp bag
crammed with your crappy mortgage
or student debt, plus the dread
from your dead-end job. Black and
Hispanic versions: to come.
The app is high but paid for
by taxing the 1%.

Wednesday, May 11, 2016

BFF* APP

Hill'ry has an app to make
the affiliative feel
affiliated: after
flipping through *I'm On Her*, *I'm
In Her*, and *I'm Beneath Her*,
it settles down with the least
bad blurred border slogan: *I'm
With Her.* Student, White Male, and
Idealist versions: to come.
The app is free with a do-
nation to her Foundation.

*duly noted:
Best Friend Forever (or until November 9)
Best Faux Friend (for Bernie realists)
Best Frenemy Forever (for Republicans who feel they have no other choice)
Boyfriend Forever (for those who think Hillary's butch)

Thursday, May 12, 2016

ALWAYS TAKE PAINS

You surely thought Trump buffoon
but vis-à-vis quiddity:
Trickster true to Yoruba
tale curling 'cross centuries:
Tortoise and Elephant, *Howl*.
You were 0 for 2, with two
strikeouts, on Inaugural
Poems for Obama. The burn
and stomach-punch from that: dis-
figuring. *Always Take Pains*.
Life goes on but you do not.

for Michael S. Harper, in memoriam
(March 18, 1938–May 7, 2016)

Friday, May 13, 2016

MR. TRUMP GOES TO WASHINGTON

or

THE TORTOISE AND THE ELEPHANT

The King took ill. He was near
death. A consultant who dwelt
in the evil forest was
consulted. The King would need
a cure made from elephant
parts cooked Right. The Tortoise knew
how to do it, how to lure
the dangerous giant to
the deep pit he'd ordered dug.
Got the job. Signifying
Monkey biz. Cloakroom dagger.

Saturday, May 14, 2016

AFTER MEETING THE DONALD, HOUSE SPEAKER PAUL RYAN CLEARS HIS THROAT (NOT HIS CONSCIENCE) AND DECLARES THAT THEY HAVE ONLY "A FEW DIFFERENCES" REMAINING....

He feels flat-chested women
are unlikely to ever
be "10s" but the most comely
among them may be "7s."
He feels women cannot be
dogs, no matter how homely.
He thinks those women are deer.
He feels unpleasant women
are not pigs, but rather, voles.
So goes the vital matter
of Saving Public Ryan.

Sunday, May 15, 2016

JOHN MILLER, FAKE PUBLICIST FOR DONALD TRUMP, PLAYED BY DONALD TRUMP HIMSELF, (BUT NOT *AS* HIMSELF) BRAGS TO A REPORTER THAT MADONNA WANTS TRUMP, THAT TRUMP TOOK CARLA BRUNI FROM MICK JAGGER (AFTER MICK TOOK HER FROM ERIC CLAPTON), THAT TRUMP SAVVILY SCREWED HIS FIRST WIFE OUT OF MILLIONS, AND THAT TRUMP HAS "A WHOLE OPEN FIELD" OF WOMEN TO PICK FROM, AND DISCUSSES OTHER MATTERS WHICH WOULD COME TO AFFECT THE PATH AND PROGRESS OF AMERICAN DEMOCRACY, AND THAT OF THE WORLD, SOME TWENTY-FIVE YEARS HENCE

or

TRUMP AS TRUMP: *I DON'T KNOW ANYTHING ABOUT IT, YOU'RE TELLING ME ABOUT IT FOR THE FIRST TIME, THIS SOUNDS LIKE ONE OF THE SCAMS, ONE OF THE MANY SCAMS, DOESN'T SOUND LIKE ME, I DON'T THINK IT WAS ME, IT DOESN'T SOUND LIKE ME, I DON'T EVEN KNOW WHAT THEY'RE TALKING ABOUT* (5/13/16)

*Well, he treats everybody
well. He's a good guy and he's
not going to hurt any-
body. I mean, he paid his
wife a great deal of money.
I'm somebody that he knows ...
I think somebody that he
trusts and likes. So I'm gonna
do this a little part-time,
then go on with my life, too.
He's got a whole open field.*

duly noted:
https://www.washingtonpost.com/politics/donald-trump-alter-ego-barron/2016/05/12/02ac99ec-16fe-11e6-aa55-670cabef46e0_story.html

Monday, May 16, 2016

THE MOST IMPORTANT ARGUMENTS
YOU HAVE ARE WITH YOURSELF

Donnybrook or dithyramb,
we slice with a snickersnee
and let the fleshy juicy
morsels flow into the stain-
less steel cups of our want. Which
kind of timocracy do
we want? Or want not at all.
Our cups are collapsible
and leak champagne's frothing fizzed
truth: if only the rich rule,
is this all amphigory?

Tuesday, May 17, 2016

PYROCLASTIC FLOW

Ash, dust, scoria, pumice.
A man invents a past. Tuff.
A man denies it. Tephra.
Founding Fathers wrote under
pseudonyms. A non-candid
candidate creates phony
publicists, falter egos,
but oh long ago. Teflon.
This lahar of news—knowing
nothing—blasts a path for our
wounded peacock of Pompeii.

for Mark Dresser

Wednesday, May 18, 2016

TIT FOR TAT

To watch the two Democrats
trade tit for tat while the wolf
(red in tooth and claw and tweet)
is at the fern-filled den door
brings to mind the old story
about reciprocated
altruism, game theory,
peer-to-peer file sharing,
optimistic unchoking,
the prisoner's dilemma, and
the Golden Bamboo Lemur.

for Billie Miro Breskin

Thursday, May 19, 2016

STUMP SPEECH

Equality and Freedom,
mongoose and cobra, you know
there are those who say this e-
lection is about a move-
ment, not business as usual.
Yes! We all know that the Nag
and Nagaina tale lives past
Rikki-Tikki-Tavi. How
to make "America First"
rhyme with "The White Man's Burden"…?
You might ask what the poem means.

Friday, May 20, 2016

ANOTHER AIRPLANE

Another bomb? Or simply
a cockpit struggle between
pilots who differed? Missile?
Malfunction? Whose flaw made this
Egyptian flying tomb? Who
made the plane a shattered sub-
human submarine? My boy
eye-rolls through college visits,
attempting to believe in
what human beings can do, what
the warm future might feel like.

for Thelonious Blue Breskin

Saturday, May 21, 2016

ENGINEERING

Whether the center holds, or
not, is best left for the ref
to decide. The assembled
boldfaced names of the Right swarm
the Facebook campus to hear
data engineers speak truth
to power. Fact: the Rapid
Unscheduled Disassembly
of their vehicle is no
fault divorce. Search for frozen
0-rings in code futile. SAD

Sunday, May 22, 2016

MANY HAPPY RETURNS

Short-fingered vulgarians
and other-proclivitied
politicians also run-
ning for president have long
coughed up their tax returns 'cause
that's how we keep score here in
this here country. One said he'd
release his soon as Monkey
African President coughed
up birth papers. Monkey did,
then other monkey didn't.

Monday, May 23, 2016

THE PLANTATION

*Going to do far better
with Hispanics than any-
one thought. I have thousands work-
ing for me. When this is o-
ver, one of my first pictures
is going to be me at
the Doral with a thousand
of my people working there,
most of whom are Hispanic
and all who love Trump.* Some own
for life. Some own by the hour.

duly noted:
http://www.nytimes.com/2016/05/22/magazine/donald-trump-primary-win.html

Tuesday, May 24, 2016

PROSAIC QUERY

What makes a dank billionaire
give millions to another
billionaire who won't spend a
lone billion of his supposed
ten to assume the polished
crown as the world's most power-
ful man, especially when
that billionaire made a proud
point of selfie self-funding
to show he would not be owned
under any circumstance?

Wednesday, May 25, 2016

MUSCLE

A squirrel with nuts. Coppers on
horseback. Flame-red muscle cars:
Camaros, Firebirds. Flag
of Mexico, shot in street.
Sleeper cells, paranoid eye
phone android de toke ville. A
rally is a car race. A
race to the brown bottom. Low
riders. Tattoos. Tear gas, skid
marks. We're Americans. We
like to blow stuff up real good.

for Jesse Nichols

Thursday, May 26, 2016

LET'S

Let's go forwards backwards. Let's
retreat into the future.
Let's not let nothing stop us.
Let's join the club that wants us.
Let's come together. Let's be
real. Let's plan to hook up in
that park we like so much we
killed all the grass with our cleats.
Let's smell it like it is, you
know, the flatulent expense
of our electioneering.

Friday, May 27, 2016

ITEMS DEPOSITED ON THE SIDEWALK, OBSERVED DURING A BRISK WALK UP THE FAR WEST SIDE OF MANHATTAN, BETWEEN 23ʳᴰ AND 47ᵀᴴ STREETS, TODAY (IMAGINE THIS HAS SOMETHING TO DO WITH THE COMING ELECTION)

One silver Lamborghini
Aventador (for washing
and detailing). One painting
crate with a multimillion-
dollar painting inside. One
brochure for resort-inspired
amenities in Zaha
Hadid's posthumous condo.
One homeless woman's epic
crap under her Banana
Republic white skirt, lifted.

Saturday, May 28, 2016

THE SECRETARY OF STATE'S NEGLIGEE

Inspector Generals inspect
ex post facto. Such licensed
high espial flenses fact
from fiction, blood from blubber.
Her knickers in a twist, bunched
awkwardly at her ankles,
she trips over the limbo
bar of her high ideals set
low. Diaphonous motives.
She just wishes she could be
left to her own devices.

duly noted:
Word Origin and History for negligee - 1756, "a kind of loose gown worn by women," from French *négligée*, noun use of fem. past participle of *négliger* "to neglect" (14c.), from Latin *neglegere* "to disregard, not heed, not trouble oneself about," also "to make light of" (see neglect (v.)). So called in comparison to the elaborate costume of a fully dressed woman of the period. Borrowed again, 1835; the modern sense "semi-transparent, flimsy, lacy dressing gown" is yet another revival, first recorded 1930. It also was used in the U.S. funeral industry mid-20c. for "shroud of a corpse." *Online Etymology Dictionary*, 2016, Douglas Harper.

Sunday, May 29, 2016

IRREVERENT WARRIORS: THE SILKIES HIKE

From the Willie Mays statue
to Ocean Beach, a hike/pub
crawl/ruck of 22 klicks
humping 22 kilos
donning silkies and downing
beers and shots at stops. Mission:
To raise awareness of Post-
Traumatic Stress Disorder,
our 22 vets (average)
who suicide each day. Flags,
body-painting optional.

duly noted:
http://sanfrancisco.eventful.com/events/silkies-hike-22-22-22-san-francisco-/E0-001-091970320-8
http://www.irreverentwarriors.com

Monday, May 30, 2016

MEMORIAL DAY

Start of summer fun: smoking
tires at Indy, beach outings,
backyard barbecues, half-off
sales, another day learning
nothing not in school. Who now
speaks the names of the lost? This
year, I'll take the kids to graves
whispering who was killed by whom
in what war when. Who we killed.
Who killed us. Who killed themselves.
I want it to hurt. It should.

Tuesday, May 31, 2016

STRANGELY THERE WAS BERNIE SANDERS, UNANNOUNCED, AT A PARADE TO THE GRAVES OF THE VETS, SOME HOURS BEFORE ATTENDING THE THUNDER / WARRIORS GAME 7 (DUB NATION SOLIDARITY)

Flanked by obvious Secrets
in sunglassed, earpieced glory,
some distance from the Spanish
cannons of two centuries past,
there he be, hunched over, bright
sunburn crowning his fading
white halo. Me: "Thank you for
speaking truth to power, but
please remember who our real
enemy is." He: "Thank you,
and I will, I promise you."

Wednesday, June 1, 2016

JUNE BABOON SWOON LOON TUNE HARPOON

If history don't repeat
itself but rhymes why in these
times do we have none but slant
and half if that? Goofy. Sleaze.
Sloppy. Grubby. Sad. Crude. Dog.
Penguin. Pocahontas. Rigged.
Fraud. Disgusting. Dumb. Puppet.
Racist. Hater. Bombed. Bad. Fail.
Boring. Garbage. Weak. Choker.
Corrupt. Troubled. Phony. Clown.
Soft. Buffoon. Total loser.

duly noted:
http://www.nytimes.com/interactive/2016/01/28/upshot/donald-trump-twitter-insults.html

Thursday, June 2, 2016

EMPTY POSSESSIONS

Look around, look around: stuff
we don't need much cluttering
the country, private storage
units abound in safety
orange and poured concrete, banging
roll-up metal-door treasure
troves. In basketball, coaches
call possessions ending in
turnovers empty. What if
this whole election ended
up being exactly that?

for Tomas Fujiwara

Friday, June 3, 2016

PRESUMPTIVE

or

A WIDOW'S PEAK TO CRACK A FURROWED BROW IN HALF

After careful study—deep
into the night for many
nights his lustrous laptop burned,
illuminating the dense
web of delicately con-
structed positions of the
presumptive nominee on
taxes, civics, domestic
affairs, foreign policy—
The Speaker of the House trum-
pets: he's the man for the job.

Saturday, June 4, 2016

GONZALO P. CURIEL

If this judge is Mexican
then I am purely Russian
and Donald Trump the grandson
of Friedrich Drumpf of Kallstadt
Germany and Mary Smith
MacLeod of Tong Scotland would
be 50/50 German
Scottish but if this country
has any balls at all it's
'cause we made ourselves anew.
Or are they called cojones?

Sunday, June 5, 2016

LOOK AT MY AFRICAN-AMERICAN OVER HERE! LOOK AT HIM! ARE YOU THE GREATEST?

Piece of cake, the candidate
sees him in a sea of white
faces in Redding, CA.
(His use of the possessive
leaves some unamused on the
Left, while the Right could care less.)
Praised next: *Slugging, cold-cocking*
protesters. *Are we having
fun?* The lectern's TRUMP sign, cock-
eyed from the start, begins to
fall, grip slipping, in the heat.

duly noted:
https://www.youtube.com/watch?v=rOYMFkFgPzk

Monday, June 6, 2016

LOOK AT MY AFRICAN-AMERICAN OVER HERE!
LOOK AT HIM! ARE YOU THE GREATEST?

If the question had only
been addressed to Muhammad
Ali the answer would ring
clear. That man taught me more style,
poetry and history,
more civics than a shuffling
ministry of school teachers.
Would that he could rope-a-dope
The Donald in Kinshasa.
Or call buffoon gorilla.
He was mine. Yours. Theirs. And ours.

for Muhammad Ali, in memoriam
(January 17, 1942–June 3, 2016)

Tuesday, June 7, 2016

TRUMP UNIVERSITY: INTRODUCTORY COURSES IN THE OTHER DEPARTMENTS

Biology: *The Penis: A Short Introduction.* Psych: *Id, Ego, Superduper-ego.* Cosmetology: *Orange Is The New White.* German Studies: *Overlooked Aspects Of All The Good The Führer Did Which He Gets No Credit For.* Earth Science: *Truth, Dare, Or Hoax?* Women's Studies: *Plastic Surgery: It's Not Too Late.*

Wednesday, June 8, 2016

THE STRUGGLE CONTINUES (MORE OR LESS)

"Inside the bitter last days
of Bernie's revolution,"
Politico's banana
peel slip dishing the flipped script
of his California FAIL.
Rage against the machine, Bern
it down. Talk about yourself
in third person. "Screw me? No,
screw you." Why choose to knife-fight?
Sorry, you're unqualified.
The Struggle, et cetera.

duly noted:
http://www.politico.com/story/2016/06/bernie-sanders-campaign-last-days-224041

Thursday, June 9, 2016

JUNE 5, 1968

Juan Romero cradled his
head, placed a rosary in
his hand. "Is everybody
okay?" the candidate asked.
"Yes, everybody's okay,"
Juan replied. The candidate
then turned his head away from
the kneeling young busboy, and
issued his final statement:
"Everything's going to be
okay." He was dead wrong. Right?

Friday, June 10, 2016

BOBBY AND BERNIE (CALIFORNIA)

No metal detector. No
stop and frisk. No cordon, fence
or shield. Only two nervous
Secret Service guys, paces
away, on Memorial
Day, when I walked up to Bern,
shook his hand, and exchanged words.
I could have done some worse thing,
easy, changing his story,
and mine. 'Twas thrilling, scary,
creepy. It's a free country.

Saturday, June 11, 2016

STEMWINDER

To watch Elizabeth rip
a certain someone a new
youknowhat is to feel fresh
air breezing, not hard blowing,
into the wobbly public
square. Fit and trim for battle,
she plays the sassy schoolmarm
who can punch above her weight.
Enough rodomontade from
unprincipled principals!
Soon we'll see her best left hook.

for Julie Breskin

Sunday, June 12, 2016

TO WAKE UP

on Sunday morning in this
sunny city, the fog cleared,
triathletes fluttering from
Alcatraz to their bikes and
feet, Amazonian green
parrots (non-natives) wheeling
gaily by my window, then
hear news that Omar Mateen
so hated to see kissing
men he murdered as many
as he could, is to feel queer.

for Todd Hosfelt

Monday, June 13, 2016

NOW, FOR THE 72 VIRGINS (IN A TWO-FOR-ONE SPECIAL, AN ISIS MUFTI HAS PROMISED 144 IF A MARTYR IS KILLED AT THE HANDS OF THE AMERICANS)

The science is not settled
as to what awaits Omar
in Heaven. The texts are in-
conclusive. But it's what he
felt that counts. He might have bet
on pure girls, *eyes like pearls*, but
could end instead with *young boys
of perpetual freshness.*
Probably what he wanted
anyway, hating himself
and all of them for wanting.

duly noted:

http://www.military.com/video/operations-and-strategy/terrorism/cleric-permits-killing-us-women-children/3776097067001
"A houri is a most beautiful young woman with a transparent body. The marrow of her bones is visible like the interior lines of pearls and rubies. She looks like red wine in a white glass. She is of white color, and free from the routine physical disabilities of an ordinary woman such as menstruation, menopause, urinal and offal discharge, child bearing and the related pollution. A houri is a girl of tender age, having large breasts which are round (pointed), and not inclined to dangle. Houris dwell in palaces of splendid surroundings."
Al-Tirmidhi (824-892) *Jami' at-Tirmidhi*

Tuesday, June 14, 2016

THE METAMORPHOSIS BUSINESS

He's a nobody. He's a customer, said the owner
of the St. Lucie Shooting
Center where Omar Mateen
bought his 9mm
semiautomatic pis-
tol and his AR-15
assault rifle. Worm into
butterfly, becoming some-
body in a single night,
then no body once again.

Wednesday, June 15, 2016

AND YET: *AND YET HE CONTINUES*
TO PRIORITIZE OUR ENEMY…

Ever since he was born (un-
fortunately) Barack Hus-
sein Obama (in Kenya
by the way) has not been one
of US. Bananas. Water-
melon. Basketball. You know.
Or he gets it better than
anybody understands.
Way he smells. Ears. Mole. People,
people say there's something wrong.
He's got something else in mind.

duly noted:
http://www.theatlantic.com/politics/archive/2016/06/trump-again-accuses-obama-of-treason/487034/

Thursday, June 16, 2016

APOPHASIS

I will not mention the man
who often rings this cracked bell
in broad speech and dripping tweet
as a way of saying some-
thing more yet less and something
less yet more than the thing it-
self he claims not to say nor
will I even point out his
cowardice or treachery
since doing so would only
give him smug satisfaction.

Friday, June 17, 2016

AND IN THE CATEGORY OF THE FIRST MAMMAL GONE EXTINCT FROM HUMAN-CAUSED CLIMATE CHANGE, THE WINNER IS .... THE BRAMBLE CAY MELOMYS (*MELOMYS RUBICOLA*).... UNFORTUNATELY, THE BRAMBLE CAY MELOMYS COULD NOT BE HERE TONIGHT, SO ACCEPTING THE AWARD FOR HER IS FELLOW AUSTRALIAN, GREAT BARRIER REEF ENTHUSIAST, AND FOX HONCHO, RUPERT MURDOCH, AC, KCSG

Whether the extensive ex-
halations of pols and pun-
dits were sufficient to cause
temperature's upward trend, or
whether our fire-making
ways, the lit match of our sheer
industry, punked the planet
just quite enough finally
is always so hard to know,
since the giant Fox tells us
the science isn't settled.

for Mark Hart III

Saturday, June 18, 2016

OBAMA IS A SPECIAL KIND OF STUPID

Exploiting a sick, evil, ideological-driven attack on Americans to further your twisted anti-Second Amendment mission ... disgusting. 15 MILLION PLUS WOMEN HAVE DECIDED TO OWN A FIREARM. YOU MIGHT CALL IT A WOMAN'S RIGHT TO CHOOSE. —Sarah Palin, Facebook post, First Amendment.

duly noted:
http://insider.foxnews.com/2016/06/17/sarah-palin-obama-special-kind-stupid

Sunday, June 19, 2016

APOPHYSIS

A garden-variety
xenophobia always
masks irregular swelling
in the body politic.
Who's to say what's unreason-
able in fear's brackish crunch?
A reason for Brexit, brunch,
Remain Calm & Carry On.
Let's watch each fresh new shooting
stalk time-lapse the horizon.
Projection. Protuberance.

Monday, June 20, 2016

MANDATORY POEM

You campaign in poetry.
You govern in prose. Cuomo
quote from thirty years ago
still good to go but look here
at the two-and-a-third job
seekers: all hammers searching
bent nails, proud of the surface,
to smash flush. Ecstatic dance
it's not. Trial balloons filled
with natural gas. Polls. Cash.
There is no poetry here.

for Zohar Atkins

Tuesday, June 21, 2016

GUN CONTROL

Bombs misdirect energy.
Sloppy. Tricky. Unready-
made. Poison's old school. Too-too.
Peaceful. Requires Chem 1.
Knives be blunt. Wet work. *Thuck thuck.*
Fists: appalling passion. Clear
crimp of self-limitation.
Elimination's process
proves plain to we, the people,
a gun's the best way to win
an argument with the world.

Wednesday, June 22, 2016

MEMO TO THE 45% OF SANDERS SUPPORTERS
WHO IN A RECENT POLL INDICATE THEY
WON'T VOTE FOR HILLARY CLINTON
(22% SAY THEY'LL VOTE TRUMP, 18% FAVOR
LIBERTARIAN GARY JOHNSON, 5% SAY OTHER)

Are you on drugs? Are you so
badly Bernt that Rage Against
The Machine is the only
band you'll play? Thinking crooked?
You know anything about
Libertarianism?
(The word takes up a whole line!)
Trump? Angry White People Sucked
In By Personality
Cult Who Want To Blow Things Up?
Sound like you? Low Blow? Reveal.

Thursday, June 23, 2016

THE SPEAKER OF OUR HOUSE, DEEP INTO THE NIGHT

Who does the Speaker speak for?
The *DONT TREAD ON ME* crowd, fear-
ful of Big Brother snuffing
their God- or Founding Father-
given right (easily con-
fused) to fondle guns under
covers, freely, and the free
Association rifles
enjoy with themselves and Right-
ful Owners, bloody well-paid
for rattlesnakes rising, or …

duly noted:
https://en.wikipedia.org/wiki/Gadsden_flag

Friday, June 24, 2016

BREXIT (HIGH TEA REMIX)

The Intolerable Acts.
1774.
A Royal Bureaucratic
Aristocracy, Brussels.
2016. Natives.
Nativism. Coloni-
alism. Other ism.
Islamism. Indians.
Alexander Hamilton.
A billionaire on Scottish
course cuts ribbons, ties, and sails.

Saturday, June 25, 2016

I WISH TO SPEAK TO YOU TODAY ABOUT THE TRAGEDY OF EUROPE (THE UNITED STATES OF EUROPE SPEECH)

Indeed, but for the fact that
the great Republic across
the Atlantic Ocean has
at length realised that the ruin
or enslavement of Europe
would involve their own fate as
well, and has stretched out hands of
succour and guidance, the Dark
Ages would have returned in
all their cruelty and squalor.
They may still return. —Churchill

duly noted:
http://www.churchill-society-london.org.uk/astonish.html

Sunday, June 26, 2016

POPULISM

Populism is sometimes
popular. Bubblegum pop,
pinpricked balloon. But sometimes
it's botulism and makes
a whole nation spasm and
curl on the cold bathroom floor
of its half-hearted regret,
and 'tween bouts of puking the
fuck up, it drools a new day,
a barker or mountebank
with a wicked, fresher tale.

Monday, June 27, 2016

COME TOGETHER, RIGHT NOW, OVER ME

As far Right and far Left grow
apart they get closer to-
gether and eventually
meet at the dark middle of
the backside of our sphere (all
things us being round and not
flat) and unite there, finding
some available Moloch
to suit their needs, and return
to the perfect toddler state:
in thrall to Mom, fed, sleeping.

duly noted:
https://en.wikipedia.org/wiki/Come_Together

Tuesday, June 28, 2016

THE OBLIGATION TOWARD THE DIFFICULT WHOLE

Automagical surprise.
Microtargeted leaners.
Psychographic voter maps.
Digital outreach sample
pack. Focus group data dump.
Trend harvest. Bias toolbox.
Protocols. Robocalls. Lawn
signs. Infrastructure reboot.
Brexpert dismissal. Code smell.
Between Philly and Pittsburgh,
PA is Alabama.

Wednesday, June 29, 2016

ATATURK AIRPORT, ISTANBUL

One: *I grabbed my family and
ran. Someone waved us into
the prayer room and hid us there.*
Two: *I thought about using
boiling tea water as a
weapon to burn the attack-
er if he found us in the
closet so my wife can run.*
Three: *My girl, my girl, my girl.
I have no other, I had
only one.* Four, Five, Six, Sev-

for Mimi Chakarova

Thursday, June 30, 2016

VISCERAL

Speaking from the gut is like
seeing with knees or smelling
from the spine. Nonetheless we
find, in his gut, the pickled
remains of beautiful deals,
chewed newspapers, stupendous-
ly tough bacteria, old
Playboy centerfolds, rusting
lunchboxes of abandoned
factories, a Thanksgiving
play costume from 4th grade, mints.

NOT SO VISCERAL

Federally-mandated
inspection of the contents
of her well-insulated
stomach cites: senior thesis
on Saul Alinsky, french fries,
Blackberry instruction man-
ual, one purple dental
dam, remnants of gift fragrance
from some ambassador *(Eau
de Entitlement),* a map
of the world, twelve talking points.

Friday, July 1, 2016

WHITE MEN

Lotta talk 'bout how white men
feel disenfranchised but last
I looked white men could still vote.
Just they ain't the only ones
no more. News Flash: Those Days, Gone.
As new polls show white men want
HIM over HER by thirty
monstrous percent, a final
solution may be called for:
a sex-change operation
and hardcore home tanning bed.

Saturday, July 2, 2016

MY COUNTRY, 'TIS OF THEE

How to be a civilian
when all around you combat-
ants crawl? Impossible Germ-
any unlikely England.
At Spanish truckstop, ponder
Regrexit. Why was I born?
Why am I living? What do
I get? What am I giving?
Jokers to the left of me,
walls to the right, here I am,
stuck in the middle with you.

for Nels Cline

Sunday, July 3, 2016

GONE FISHIN'

Saturday, July 23, 2016

UNCONVENTIONAL
(*I WENT BACK TO OHIO BUT MY CITY WAS GONE*)

To summarize: Immigrants
roam free while in foreign lands
data roaming is so dear
facts get manufactured (jobs!)
to suit his meaty hot dog
vowels. Cops shot but blacks not.
Law and Order. Law and/or
else. Shots of Fear, knocked back. I:
I alone can fix it. The
face of Herr Drumpf, in full cry,
was redder than expected.

for Ellen Darst

Sunday, July 24, 2016

THE KAINE MUTINY

The livid Sandernistas
who barely see the point of
jumping on Hillary's list-
less ship, doldrummed, adrift in
internationally sanc-
tioned waters, now are beside
themselves (and beside those selves
they are besides, sharks) over
the pick of this white male man
who might rudder right. Where are
those strawberries? Cue: steel balls.

Monday, July 25, 2016

BERNED

Was Bernie born last night? Acts
it. Lifelong INDEPENDENT
(all respect to *that*, brother!)
he "becomes" a Dem to run
for Prez (as if Born Again
in turgid, gator'd water)
only to later act *shocked,*
shocked that the Being Powers
of Dem Nat Com behind scenes
favor lady who's punched and
been punched for them her whole life.

for Isabel Breskin

duly noted:
http://www.politifact.com/truth-o-meter/article/2016/feb/23/bernie-sanders-democrat/

Tuesday, July 26, 2016

AMERICA FIRST

You only take the smallest
sips of water while sewing
His shirts because bathroom breaks
cause missed quotas. Every day
a wall of heat and cruel supes
and a buck sixty an hour.
The company food makes you
sick, so for lunch you reach through
the fence for something better,
at the big Protexsa plant
in Choloma, Honduras.

duly noted:
https://www.buzzfeed.com/karlazabludovsky/meet-the-workers-who-sewed-donald-trump-clothing-for-a-few-d

Wednesday, July 27, 2016

BUBBA

Look, we know they fucked at least
once—Chelsea clearly appears
clapping in her luxury
box a 50/50 blend
of them two. He gives his speech,
attempting for a sort of
valiant modesty, his first
official try-out for First
Gentleman. His once plumply
pink cheeks have hollowed, but he
still's got rhythm, and knows *how*.

Thursday, July 28, 2016

HACK

If only the IRS
dam leaked like the DNC's,
then, to counter Trump's rimming
whiff of Putin's arse, and his
polite request that Russia
hack more of her sweet nothings,
she would only have to ask
the Chinese military
(who "made up" global warming)
to locate the last thirty
years of his happy returns.

Friday, July 29, 2016

GONE PADDLIN'

Sunday, August 7, 2016

GOLD STAR QUESTION

    It was a picture that moved
the Secretary of State
to come out of the closet
for Obama in Oh Eight:
a mother with her head on
the headstone of her son's grave.
Not Ghazala with her son
but another Khan in stone:
Kareem Rashad Sultan Khan.
Do you want a big country?
Or do you want a small one?

    duly noted:
https://www.youtube.com/watch?v=jXWqX_O4BKY

Monday, August 8, 2016

JULIAN ASSANGE

could be zipped in a "Diplo-
matic Body Bag" and snuck
to Ecuador so rapt, un-
known to Authorities, but
thermal imaging of said
bag at Heathrow would reveal
his heat and allow Author-
ities to "seize the concealed
Assange." If only he'd kept
his member wrapped in Stockholm:
the blasted condom, which leaked.

Tuesday, August 9, 2016

THE BIG HOUSE (LOCK HER UP)

According to modern fact-
checking methodologies,
Hillary bends, folds, scrunches,
tampers with and taffy-pulls
the truth pretty much inside
the norms set by her fellow
class of politicians. If
you jailed her for some such crimes
the joint would be so lousy
with pols (and their molls) you'd have
to short-circuit her sentence.

Wednesday, August 10, 2016

WHAT TRUMP REALLY MEANT

I mean, give me a break, o-
kay? But they (they are so dis-
honest, most, most of them, be-
lieve me folks, and they lie, most-
ly lie) but I see now man-
y people, people have look-
ed at this and they are say-
ing the same thing, many peo-
ple are saying that there's noth-
ing there, so much, to be hon-
est it's unbelievable.

duly noted:
https://www.yahoo.com/news/many-people-saying-trump-tweet-000000450.html

Thursday, August 11, 2016

THE RIGHTS OF "SECOND AMENDMENT PEOPLE" TO TAKE CERTAIN THINGS INTO THEIR OWN HANDS AFTER THE ELECTION IN CASE THINGS DON'T TURN OUT RIGHT

As prime Trump surrogate—who
stiffened his sclerotic spine
spinning that The Donald's quack
about "Second Amendment
People" bore nary a hint
of Hillary's assassi-
nation—I fear Rudy G.
may have revealed more than he
wished when he uttered: *With a
crowd like that, if that's what they
thought he'd meant, they'd have gone wild.*

https://www.nytimes.com/2016/08/10/us/politics/donald-trump-hillary-clinton.html?_r=0

http://www.businessinsider.com/giuliani-trump-violence-clinton-second-amendment-2016-8

Friday, August 12, 2016

AFTER THEY FOUNDED ISIS

A lot of spare time on hand
because ISIS (or ISIL
if you will) was so darn up
for the job at hand they (Hil'
& Hussein) did not have to
do much more in the Traitor
Department. Still, Barack found
time to poop on the Bible
and Monster-slash-Devil Hil'
drop-kicked kittens into the
brew pots of liberal witches.

duly noted:
http://www.cnn.com/2016/08/11/politics/donald-trump-hugh-hewitt-obama-founder-isis/

Saturday, August 13, 2016

IF

If he wins, history will
show current events to mean
X, Y, and Z. If she wins,
history will pour those same
events into the fiery
forge from which A, B, and C
get smashed and hammered. Yet yet
the events didn't differ.
Explanation rules harshly
in *Ex Post Facto*'s kingdom.
The root of forge: fabricate.

for Marc Vincenz

Sunday, August 14, 2016

TALK / SHOW

If you took all the Blacks and
Jews out of America
you'd be left with Germany
without the timely trains or
a single singer who could
raise his voice to adoring
crowds who could show what love is
for who would erase larger
problems stop Hispandering
erect magic Lego walls
put the ouch back in Auschwitz

for Jeff Tweedy

Monday, August 15, 2016

BOLT

Speed appeals. Blocks, shoes, starter's
gun. Sprayed-on suit and green *Go*
tone in the 50 free. Then
splash and dash or forty plus
strides to glory. Finis. Lean
mean time machine. But neither
stopwatch nor sundial sweeps slow
enough to measure the ex-
cruciating crawl of our
elective duodecu-
ple Ironman Triathlon.

for Mary Halvorson

Tuesday, August 16, 2016

IDEOLOGICAL SCREENING TEST
(*I CALL IT EXTREME VETTING*)

I call it extreme, EXTREME vetting. Like: *Do you believe shariah law should supplant American law?* Further: *Do you believe in our Constitution or support bigotry and hatred?* In truth her papers have always been proper (immunizations too) but no way could my cockapoo answer these questions.

duly noted:
http://abcnews.go.com/Politics/donald-trump-proposes-extreme-vetting-immigrants-ideological-screening/story?id=41392682

Wednesday, August 17, 2016

DEAR OMAROSA MANIGAULT, DIRECTOR OF AFRICAN-AMERICAN OUTREACH FOR THE TRUMP CAMPAIGN, WHOSE BROTHER AND FATHER WERE VICIOUSLY MURDERED

Never watched *The Apprentice*.
Never read your tome *The Bitch Switch*. Perhaps I should. I know you blew up in *Fear Factor*, *The Surreal Life, Oprah, Girls Behaving Badly*: all good!!!
But *The Ultimate Merger* dating game show left you with no one, ultimately. Now you must be the loneliest woman in America.

duly noted:
https://en.wikipedia.org/wiki/Omarosa
https://en.wikipedia.org/wiki/The_Ultimate_Merger
http://www.omarosa.com

Thursday, August 18, 2016

CLARENCE JONES

In his hunt for the last pissed-
off white man without college
degree in a swing state not
yet yelling *Trump That Bitch*, he
choppers through the sagging poll
night to the Rockies' Eastern
Front, to a lone, proud cabin
in moonlight, only to find
the owner passed years ago,
might have indeed been black, and
cared solely for cutlery.

for Ed Ruscha

duly noted:
http://edruscha.com/works/clarence-jones/

Friday, August 19, 2016

STATUESQUE

In this haunted house August
we need industrial strength
epoxy just to keep fear
glued to the curb. Trump nude (or
is he naked?) comes into
our pubic square, unashamed.
The government clears its deep
throat, utters: *NYC Parks
stands firmly against any
unpermitted erection,
no matter how small.* Ballsy!

duly noted:
http://dangerousminds.net/comments/nude_donald_trump_statue_glued_to_the_ground_in_several_cities

Saturday, August 20, 2016

AND AT THE END OF FOUR YEARS, I GUARANTEE YOU THAT I WILL GET OVER NINETY-FIVE PERCENT OF THE AFRICAN-AMERICAN VOTE. I PROMISE YOU!!!

*What do you have to lose by
trying something new, like Trump?
What do you have to lose? You're
living in poverty. Your
schools are no good. You have no
jobs. Fifty-eight percent of
your youth is unemployed. What
the hell do you have to lose?*
Why, de Cadillacs and de
welfare and watermelon,
Massa Trump, 'spose dat be it.

duly noted:
https://www.theguardian.com/us-news/2016/aug/20/what-do-you-have-to-lose-donald-trump-appeals-for-black-vote

Sunday, August 21, 2016

MISDIRECTION PLAY

There's one where the QB fake-
pitches left to a trailing
halfback then hands the pigskin
to the fullback slanting right
through the middle of the line.
When Trump talks not with, not to,
not even at black voters,
(while appearing to do just
that) he's really speaking to
suburban white women who
self-identify as fair.

Monday, August 22, 2016

MEANWHILE

… back at the ranch, the roundup
of the Boss's emails keeps
greenhorn cowpokes and seasoned
vaqueros tied in Nots. In
spangled leather poncho with
studs that match his eyes, Gaucho
Mook rides in on his mighty
dachshund, dismounts, and bassoons:
"Them critters get loose, you got
to turn the dadgummed forest
upside down to shake 'em free."

Tuesday, August 23, 2016

FORTUNATE SONS

Let's all agree the crown prince
of Bahrain or Bono could
hitch a ride on Hillary's
coattails whether her server
served the Republic, for which
it stands, or the Foundation
with its rebar-stiffening
billions. But John Fogerty?
Must we grant all such reports
credence? Drip. Flooded bayou …
or by her. Who'll stop the reign?

for Lance Donenberg

duly noted:
https://www.youtube.com/watch?v=iQqHzPzQsMg

Wednesday, August 24, 2016

DIRTY LAUNDRY (THE AGITATE CYCLE, WHEN THINGS COME CLEAN)

Exhausted boxers retreat
to rough-stooled corners. Tighty
whities thrown down the chute stay
down for the count. The rainbow
coalition of Pantone
swatch pantsuits begs with bleach for
another day. Fragrance-free
agents, spin doctors, two cups
of phlegm. A raven coughs up
a thong made from the finest
petrochemicals and lace.

Thursday, August 25, 2016

CALLING PROXIMA B, ORBITING RED DWARF PROXIMA CENTAURI

Oh, Proxima b, as you
Doppler around your parent,
so cuddly close to our own,
we're told today of your Gold-
ilocks state, not too hot nor
too cold, so our readers want
to know: do hanging chads fall
up rather than down given
your laws? Do your creatures vote
or hatch new leaders? Do you
have polls, or rate things by stars?

for Katie Paterson

Friday, August 26, 2016

COLLEGE TOUR (REDUX)

or

LIVES OF THE PRESIDENTS

At Lewis & Clark, we learned
of all the collegial things
Monica Lewinsky learned.
Today, at Occidental
(nicknamed Oxy without the
contin) we learned what poly
sci classes Barack dug when
not protesting apartheid.
Tomorrow, down the road some
at Whittier, we'll look for
Tricky Dick's frosh graffiti.

Saturday, August 27, 2016

C

Back in the day, Fred & Son
would make sure rental apart-
ments were available to
those whose outermost layer
was fair enough. That smelled right
to them as businessmen. They
owned the buildings, after all,
so they should rent to whom they
pleased. The apps of others, whose
money was not green enough,
were marked in a special way.

for John Chiatello

duly noted:
https://www.nytimes.com/2016/08/28/us/politics/donald-trump-housing-race.html

Sunday, August 28, 2016

TOLERANCES

A structured absence is a
presence. Turbo-injecting
empathy into every
conversation slows the pace
to STOP. The Dean of Students
bores an expensive padded
tunnel under the highway
of ideas, calls it a
safe space and calls it a day.
Let the wound-licking begin.
Rainbows, unicorns, justice.

Monday, August 29, 2016

DEPORTATION / FORCE

Taking ten or twelve million
people out of the country
because they are not legal
might seem an unseemly act
to some but would be the best
Government Jobs Program in
history 'cause you would need
quite a crew to do the job.
It's not like you could just rack
them on overhead railed hooks
like slaughterhouse carcasses.

Tuesday, August 30, 2016

ONCE AGAIN, WE VENTURE INTO HUMA ABEDIN AND THE CROTCH OF WEINER

There's nothing wrong with being
a Body Woman. Escort.
Agent. Valet. Butler. Shield.
Squeezer of Blackberries. Beard.
Shadow. Starfish. Gatekeeper.
Wardrobe Consultant. Random
Name Generator. Blender.
Idea Person. But, but,
at some point she would need to
become a Swiss Army Knife,
free to use all devices.

Wednesday, August 31, 2016

MEXICAN HAT DANCE

This dance is a lively dance
that will raise the heart rate. Ask
students to take a heart rate
before the dance and after.
Talk about the benefits
of the dance on cardio-
respiratory system.
Men should wear an ornate cow-
boy suit. Women should wear fringed
blouses, flowing skirts, and shawls.
This dance is a courting dance.

for Nina Taschian

Thursday, September 1, 2016

CRIMINAL ALIENS

The aliens of my youth
wore green poly pullovers
and warbled helium-voiced
on afterschool TV by
vibrating face-slits shaped like
AMC Pacers. Scary
slash funny. You know. *Danger,
Will Robinson!!!* But these free
buffalo-roaming brown ones
Trump talks up at rallies are
a whole different animal.

Friday, September 2, 2016

270

Mesmerizing in its stark
lush beauty, the number swans
before us, sashaying down
the grand maroon stair before
stopping to check its raccoon
gaze in a silver compact,
adjusting a pile of looped
pearls plunging into shadows
of perfumed décolletage. Ah,
The Number. Stunning. Pure. Of
days. Since. Her last press conference.

Saturday, September 3, 2016

THE JUICIEST BITS

or

THE TWELVE JUICIEST BITS FROM THE FBI'S CLINTON REPORT ACCORDING TO *POLITICO*'S NICK GASS, ONLY ONE ABOUT BLEACHBIT AND ONLY ONE MISSING

[Redacted] *Oh Shit* moment.
Trusted judgment of others.
Breaking, smashing with hammer.
Powell's BlackBerry Warning.
Apple Server Turnover.
The meaning of "(C)." Alpha?
Blasé drone strike secrecy.
Spear-phishing porn messages.
Goog' vulnerability.
The Fall: subsequent blood clot.
A prodigious Blumenthal.

duly noted:
http://www.politico.com/story/2016/09/best-of-clinton-fbi-report-227692

Sunday, September 4, 2016

HATING HILLARY

Each day a Field Trip away
from school: the mingy yellow
busses caterpillaring
the front play yard (with its half-
mast flag and chain-link fence) slump
open-doored, ever-ready
to take us to some blessed
nonschool place praised by teachers
as somehow helping us be-
come aware of the secret
dark teeming world around us.

Monday, September 5, 2016

LABOR

To plant and pick the stone fruit
to imagine the machines
and set them loose inside plants
and offices and upon
the land making rivers flow
backwards or stop when we say
stop building buildings for sleep
and for the thrumming sweating
machines for stocking things for
taking tickets the writers
of code and cherry pickers

Tuesday, September 6, 2016

LADY CAB DRIVER (THE WORLD'S FIRST PERFECT ONE-PERSON FOCUS GROUP)

To O'Hare on Labor Day.
Cigarettes, yes. Bible, yes.
Cross on rearview mirror, yes.
Climate-change denier, yes.
Rush on the radio, sure.
Conspiracy theorist, 'course.
(*Sneaky Rahm* is selling the
city's water to Israel.)
She had everything in her
short of General Jack Ripper's
precious bodily fluids.

Wednesday, September 7, 2016

USA FREEDOM KIDS

Spangly flag costumes awhirl,
Bianca, Alexis and
Izzy sang and danced their way
into the patriotic
viral heart of the inter-
webs last winter. Now stumbling
over a string of broken
promises and stolen swag,
they're suing the Trump campaign.
Sample song lyric: *Deal from
strength or get crushed every time.*

duly noted:
https://www.youtube.com/watch?v=vPRfP_TEQ-g
http://www.thedailybeast.com/articles/2016/09/06/usa-freedom-girls-sue-trump-campaign-for-stiffing-them.html

Thursday, September 8, 2016

FIELD GENERAL

A mixed-race QB who takes
a knee during the anthem
is not as plain dangerous
as one who can't read a blitz
or find his secondary
or tertiary options
in a two-minute drill. Free
speech in the home of the brave.
A toy soldier in hairspray
helmet spews: *Generals Reduced
To Rubble.* Specifics too.

for Brian Goldman

Friday, September 9, 2016

APPROVAL RATINGS

Donald is prone to finger
Vlad's approval rating as
proof of not just strength but good-
ness. (82% is
mighty good compared to O-
bama.) But Vlad's a piker
next to Benito, who scored
a perfect 100%,
and Adolf, approved by some
150%,
subject to rounding errors.

for Scott Gordon

Saturday, September 10, 2016

TWO SHOTS OF TRUMP, BEER CHASERS (JANUARY AND SEPTEMBER)

I could stand in the middle of Fifth Avenue and shoot somebody and I wouldn't lose voters, O.K.? It's, like, incredible! … / … She could walk into this arena right now and shoot somebody with 20,000 people watching right smack in the middle of the heart and she wouldn't be prosecuted, O.K.?

duly noted:
http://www.snopes.com/donald-trump-fifth-avenue-comment/
http://www.mediaite.com/online/trump-hillary-could-literally-shoot-somebody-and-she-wouldnt-be-prosecuted/

Sunday, September 11, 2016

BEAUTIFUL DESTROYERS

With Iran, when they circle
our beautiful destroyers
with their little boats and they
make gestures at our people
that they shouldn't be allowed
to make, they will be shot out
of the water. On this day,
as we fly free above great
rivers, let's remember how
easy it is for fertile
valleys to fry into dust.

for Julian Charrière

Monday, September 12, 2016

BASKET CASE?

Bring your marketing basket
to the market, your basket
of Hollywood and hedge fund
swells to your posh ballroom. You
have your Zuni and three-point
baskets, your baskets of moon-
light and complaint. You sure got
your *deplorable* basket
teed up for pulpy attack
ads, as you totter stumbling
into your woven handlers.

for Sukanya Rajaratnam

duly noted:
http://www.npr.org/2016/09/10/493427601/hillary-clintons-basket-of-deplorables-in-full-context-of-this-ugly-campaign

Tuesday, September 13, 2016

ADJECTIVES

You could pick any number
to describe people (or *folks*
as they are sometimes called) who
would make a craven cretin
the most powerful man in
the world, who thinks women pigs,
his daughter fuckable, who
pantomimes the handicapped,
shovels glitz on mirrors, hates
with a bully's cowardice:
deplorable might be one.

Wednesday, September 14, 2016

AND ONCE AGAIN, THE DREAM OF A BETTER WORLD

Fred Sandback wrote *illusion
is equivalent to real-
ity*. If we stretch the truth
from floor to ceiling, from Point
A to Point Z, fuzzy lines
form a freakonomics space
where meager means produce ripe
gardens of overflowing
plenty with no inside, no
outside, and all share. Please note
though there are holes in what's real.

for Greg Lulay

Thursday, September 15, 2016

BEFORE THEY WERE SURROGATES, THEY WERE HUNTING LEGENDS (DONALD JR. AND ERIC GO BIG, ON VACATION, IN THE AFRICAN BUSH)

While sis preferred nose and boob
jobs, her bros' intersection
at the corner of nature
and knife was more along lines
of sport: bumping off kudu,
croc, Cape buffalo, civet,
waterbuck, elephant and
leopard, for big fun. Junior
tweeted: "I AM A HUNTER
I don't hide from that. I HUNT
& EAT game." They clean up good.

for Cynthia Moss & Betsy Swart

duly noted:
http://gothamist.com/2012/03/13/photos_donald_trump_sons_awesome_at.php - photo-2
The Trump sons paid $2,795 to kill the kudu and $1,997 to kill the waterbuck. List prices for the elephant, crocodile, civet, cape buffalo and leopard were not available.

Friday, September 16, 2016

O CANADA

The True North strong and free calls
but it's tough to grab the phone
just now and say *Let's trek through
sticky tar sands to Great Slave
Lake.* Ice roads might chill fever
polls cause, but Vancouver is
Northwest Province of China
and Logan Couture and Kris
Davis took talents South years
back, so back to drawing board.
Not our home or native land.

for Nate Radley

Saturday, September 17, 2016

THE LIFE AND DEATH AND LIFE AND LIFE AND LIFE AND DEATH OF BIRTHERISM

Black guy black guy black guy black
I lost hundreds of friends on
9/11 I'm 6'3"
Obama founded ISIS
Madonna wanted to date
Black guy black guy black guy black
I saw thousands of Muslims
in Jersey City cheering
as the towers came down I
was against the Iraq War
Black guy black guy white lie black

Sunday, September 18, 2016

DOMINANCE RITUALS

To impress rivals, males seeking to rise in the dominance hierarchy perform spectacular displays: stamping, slapping the ground, dragging branches, throwing rocks. The more vigorous and imaginative the display, the faster the individual is likely to rise in the hierarchy. —Jane Goodall

Monday, September 19, 2016

FIRST AMERICAN FRIED CHICKEN (TODAY'S YELP REVIEWS)

1. Best pressure cooker cooked chicken on the east coast! 2. Wondering if this is now closed. 3. Just ordered the god is great combo meal … not bad actually. 4. Right under our nose people. How bout no one eats here ever again?
5. The place is a bomb! 6. I recommend the pulled pork sandwich or bacon double …

duly noted:
http://time.com/4500673/ahmad-rahami-first-american-fried-chicken-yelp-reviews/

Tuesday, September 20, 2016

SECURITAS (A NORMAL SATURDAY)

Dad, I'm going to the mall:
words poured like water thousands
of times a day: clear, cool, bored:
To buy a new iPhone: natch:
is jackless phone halal or
haram?: the Koran speaks not:
to Crossroads Center, St. Cloud:
The Cloud, cloud anger storage:
then Dahir Ahmed Adan:
computing: stabbing: wearing
his Securitas costume.

duly noted:
https://www.theguardian.com/us-news/2016/sep/20/minnesota-stabbing-dahir-ahmed-adan-college-security-guard

Wednesday, September 21, 2016

AHMAD KHAN RAHAMI

or

LIVES OF THE POETS (THWARTED DIVISION)

Gashing your brother don't make
you a terrorist. Just makes
you a brother. Your dad got
mad you fathered a baby
girl with that Dominican
ex-girlfriend not thinking of
the music and food that might
come out of her. Your pal from
Sonia's Beauty Color Ex-
press says you wanted to be
a poet. Our bombs hurt less.

Thursday, September 22, 2016

ON THE MATTER OF PROPER POLICING: (WHAT DID I DO TO BE SO) BLACK AND BLUE?

Swing low, sweet Charlotte. Aim high.
Even the mouse ran from my
house they laugh at you and scorn
Your truth, my truth, and the truth.
Life's just a thorn my heart is
torn why was I born what did
Book or gun, gun or book, gun.
My only sin is in my
skin what did I do to be
Black on black, blue on black, blue.
Swing low, sweet Charlotte. Aim high.

for Henry Threadgill

duly noted:
(Armstrong) https://www.youtube.com/watch?v=-vDm1lomVHU
(Wilson) https://www.youtube.com/watch?v=O88CyDeaVps
Waters) https://www.youtube.com/watch?v=5ELb0dQiV5w
(*Ain't Misbehavin'*) https://www.youtube.com/watch?v=Bm7dgOz-3Oc
(Bland) https://www.youtube.com/watch?v=vtvYqL8KQ44
(Ellington) https://www.youtube.com/watch?v=CsA04-sh67k
(Rawls) https://www.youtube.com/watch?v=tWisszu6EnI
(Armstrong) https://www.youtube.com/watch?v=2LDPUfbXRLM
(White Hand) https://www.youtube.com/watch?v=Ub9djL15Snw

Friday, September 23, 2016

DESTINY VAN WINKLE

Destiny Van Winkle stars
in a reality show:
Lockup: Extended Stay. There's
nothing more real than prison
except prison with ratings.
A cellmate cornrows her hair.
She used to trick. Get in cars.
Give plasma. Western Union.
As soon as she leaves the joint,
she'll smoke whatever crack she
can find in reality.

Saturday, September 24, 2016

GARY JOHNSON

could be the third-string flanker
on that '70s football
team, smoking weed before games
knowing he'd never play. Don't
harsh his mellow with climate
change talk, Aleppo, blah blah.
Nine percent of us say we'll
vote for the guy who exhaled,
In billions of years, the sun's
going to actually grow
and encompass the earth, right?

duly noted:
http://www.deathandtaxesmag.com/304439/gary-johnson-climate-change-is-okay-because-the-sun-will-swallow-the-earth-someday-anyway/

Sunday, September 25, 2016

JILL STEIN

I postulate you at home
this Sunday not preparing
for the big debate, free to
religiously do Green things:
recycling feelings, weaving
hemp bicycles, composting
sweaters worn through bitter in-
door winters, asking whether
energy in dogs' wagging
tails might somehow be harnessed
for the greater good, napping.

Monday, September 26, 2016

FORENSIC

or

ANTICIPATING THE FIRST PRESIDENTIAL DEBATE

Of or before the forum.
Anthropology, dentistry, entomology, pathology, botany, biology, DNA profiling, chemistry, linguistics, statistics, accounting, toxicology, arts, psychology, ballistics, skid marks, mug shots, fingerprints, mud. He Said, She Said, He Said, She …

duly noted:
http://www.americanforensics.org/what.html

Tuesday, September 27, 2016

POST-DEBATE HEADER:
TRUMP AGAIN SLAMS FORMER MISS UNIVERSE OVER WEIGHT
SUB-HEAD:
CANDIDATE PREVIOUSLY CALLED ALICIA MACHADO "MISS PIGGY" AND "MISS HOUSEKEEPING"

or

AS WE CONSIDER THE BEAUTY STANDARDS OF RED DWARFS, BLACK HOLES, SUPERNOVAS, COMETS, QUASARS, PLANETS, SOLAR SYSTEMS AND INDEED GALAXIES OF THE UNIVERSE, MIGHT WE BE OPEN TO THE POSSIBILITY THAT SOMEWHERE, ON ONE OR MORE SUCH BODIES, THICKER THIGHS, WIDER WAISTS, CHUBBIER ARMS, BIGGER BUTTS, AND GENERALLY MORE ZAFTIG CONFIGURATIONS GRACING CERTAIN FEMALES MAY BE CONSIDERED PRIZE ATTRIBUTES AND NOT SHAMEFUL DISQUALIFIERS, BASED, OF COURSE, ON LOCAL VALUES ONLY

*That person was a Miss U-
niverse person, and she was
the worst we ever had. She
was impossible. She was
the winner, and, you know, she
gained a massive amount of
weight, and it was a real prob-
lem. A real problem. Not on-
ly that, her attitude. So
Hillary went back into
the years and she found this girl.*

duly noted:
http://www.politico.com/story/2016/09/full-transcript-first-2016-presidential-debate-228761

Wednesday, September 28, 2016

FACT-CHECK

Nature abhors a moron.
Or: Every normal man must
be tempted, at times, to spit
upon his hands, hoist the black
flag, and begin slitting throats.
Immorality is the
morality of those who
are having a better time.
Truth would quickly cease to be
stranger than fiction, once we
got as used to it. —Mencken.

for Dave Hickey

Thursday, September 29, 2016

THIRD PARTIES OF THE NIGHT (MILLENNIAL REMIX)

Wasted yet prickly, you end
up under the wobbly ping-
pong table on the ratty
shag carpet with a guy who
can't remember his own name
or the names of anyone
he digs abroad as much as
the next guy but unless you
want to do him best to go
home with that boring gal from
the boring second party.

Friday, September 30, 2016

ON THE QUESTION OF FORMING A MORE PERFECT UNION, WITH A MOMENTARY ASIDE AS TO THE NATURE OF PROGRESS, AS A GENERAL IDEA AND IDEAL

How could fifty-thousand gen-
erations of hunting and
gathering, followed by five-
hundred generations of
agriculture, science, and
urban life, lead us to this:
the world's most advanced nation,
in rapt contemplation of
awarding its most awesome
prize and challenge, to this soft,
wet, cruel, mewling human fart?

Saturday, October 1, 2016

ECONOMY OF MEANS

The sucky economy
section of the plane may be
worthy of peanut "tasting
menu" standup jokes but those
of us up here today must
know of our privilege: lofted
in a metal and plastic
tube high above the sweatless
but sweating out-of-work steel
workers, longshoremen, and bug-
gy whip makers, RIP.

for Ron Saint Germain

Sunday, October 2, 2016

ALWAYS TOWARDS CAKEWALK

Observe: the country as real
estate. Net Operating
Losses snowdrift into yuge
piles of money burying
the avalanched innocents,
while all the charged whites and blacks
of the piano pinwheel and
blur into a harmonic
whole. This ones-and-zeroes land-
scape, where zeroes count for some-
thing, glides always towards cakewalk.

for Craig Taborn

Monday, October 3, 2016

TRACKING POLLS
(NORTHEAST REGIONAL #141)

If we didn't have a track
we'd be off track. Ribbon rail
gleams with a future we want
but can't begin to know. Dreams
die daily upon every
alarm. Rusted trackside wreck-
age speeds by in the splintered
fall sun. Hillbilly hero-
in to blame for all these lives
up on blocks. We're all riding
forwards backwards. Past, past, past.

Tuesday, October 4, 2016

AFTER PLAYING FOOTBALL, TENNIS, GOLF, AND SQUASH, THE CANDIDATE REMEMBERS HIS FIVE DRAFT DEFERMENTS DURING THE VIETNAM WAR (*I HAD A DOCTOR THAT GAVE ME A LETTER—A VERY STRONG LETTER ON THE HEELS. YOU KNOW, IT WAS DIFFICULT FROM THE LONG-TERM WALKING STANDPOINT*)

or

PTSD (NOBODY WOULD BELIEVE IT)

When you talk about the men-
tal health problems, when people
come back from war and combat—
and they see things that maybe
a lot of folks in this room
have seen many times over
and you're strong and you can han-
dle it, but a lot of peo-
ple can't handle it. They see
events that you couldn't see
in a movie. Nobody . . .

duly noted:
https://www.washingtonpost.com/news/post-politics/wp/2016/10/03/trump-suggests-military-members-with-mental-health-issues-arent-strong-and-cant-handle-it/

Wednesday, October 5, 2016

MEEP MEEP SHEEP SHEEP VEEP LEAP

Bonds of understanding. Stop
& Frisk would be a big mis-
take. Scourge of gun violence. At
the risk of agreeing with
you let me say this. Please. Catch
& Release. Small Potatoes.
Deportation Nation. Build
a wall. Focus: criminal
aliens. They will all be
gone. Mostly it's been a lack
of leadership. Orlando!

Thursday, October 6, 2016

YOU WAKE UP ASLEEP

I wake up in Chicago.
The river's running backwards
and in the Public Hotel
hall Chris Christie impishly
jiggles about wearing a
red Speedo—Pump Room steak knife
flashing in one hand, the head
of Katy Tur dripping from
the other. A yellow sky,
thunder. The seiche-mad lake swirls
small perch into the lobby.

Friday, October 7, 2016

STORM SURGE (MATTHEW 28:19)

Alligators abandon
honey holes. Republicans
insist science is *belief*
not truth, like faith in trickle-
down economics even
though data disproves belief.
Rain is captured by robot
cameras, streets signs dance Devo:
weather porn a dopamine
delight for shut-ins. Watch, watch.
A life in Haiti means less.

for Ches Smith

duly noted:
https://www.youtube.com/watch?v=K4d7gsgBEhE

Saturday, October 8, 2016

YOU CAN DO ANYTHING (BILLY BUSH BANTER)

or

DAYS OF OUR LIVES

In all the life instructions
Mama and Big Daddy Drumpf
funneled down to The Donald
before sending him off to
toy-soldier military
boarding school, he must have missed
the one about pussies not
being designed for grabbing.
But he did learn well the one
about using mints to stanch
his pie hole's horrid bouquet.

duly noted:
https://www.accesshollywood.com/articles/access-hollywood-archival-footage-reveals-vulgar-trump-comments-2005/

Sunday, October 9, 2016

THE MIRRORED BALLROOM

When I try to type pussy-
gate my louche private email
sheriff still autocorrects
to pussycat. Will there be
such a self-editing scheme
for We The People, or will
our Sunday School TMZ
politics roll another
gutter ball? At the slivered
alley our league calls home, fore-
play up against the dumpster.

Monday, October 10, 2016

THE DAY AFTER / TRAINWRECK
(THE SECOND DEBATE)

A thousand baboons knuckling
rough a thousand keyboards might
have a better, cleaner shot
at creating a linked train
of thought—ideas coupled
neatly behind a mental
engine of tractive power—
than, alas, Herr Drumpf, blowing
off steam, sidetracked, on the spur
where the circus train hunkers
when the circus is in town.

duly noted:
http://www.politico.com/story/2016/10/2016-presidential-debate-transcript-229519

Tuesday, October 11, 2016

ADDITIONAL USES FOR SPECIAL PROSECUTORS (GRAB 'EM BY THE LAPELS)

Kathy Karzan in 6th grade
passed notes with Richie Plonsker,
not me. Lock Her Up! Mrs.
Stunkel dumped me in the low-
est reading group when facts showed
I read gooder than most. Jail
time for old Stinky Stunkel.
Peter Thiel and John Paulson:
hmm … two semi-smart billion-
aires licking Trump's purse: Death By
Clubbing (at late night gay bars).

Wednesday, October 12, 2016

24 HOUR PARTY PEOPLE (GRAND OLD PARTY DEMIX)

To watch a wild party come
apart at the unseemlies
is a spectacle worthy
of David Attenborough,
crouched in a blind or wading
through piranha. He would know
that previously seemly
behavior was only a
ruse anyway, a Darwin-
ian adaptation. Not
what it seemed. Magnificent!

Thursday, October 13, 2016

I'LL TELL YOU THE FUNNIEST

or

INSPECTOR GENERAL (AND SO I SORT OF GET AWAY WITH THINGS LIKE THAT)

*I'll go backstage before a
show and everyone's getting
dressed and ready and every-
thing else. And you know, no men
are anywhere. And I'm al-
lowed to go in because I'm
the owner of the pageant.
And therefore, I'm "inspecting"
it. You know I'm inspecting
it. You know they're standing there
with no clothes. And so I sort …*

for Anjelique Payne (Miss Colorado Teen USA, 1994)

duly noted:
http://www.cnn.com/2016/10/08/politics/trump-on-howard-stern/
http://www.rollingstone.com/politics/features/timeline-of-trumps-creepiness-while-he-owned-miss-universe-w444634

Friday, October 14, 2016

CREEPY CLOWN

Isn't it rich? Isn't it
queer? The family values part-
y so late in its career …
which hates victimization
trope key to "political
correctness" but now sports pro-
fessional victim / victim-
monger as standard bearer.
Always someone else's fault.
Isn't it bliss? Don't you love
farce? Send … Don't bother, he's here.

for Don Ruhman

Saturday, October 15, 2016

AFTER PAINFUL SCALP REDUCTION SURGERY TO REMOVE A BALD SPOT, HE CONFRONTS HIS WIFE, WHO HAD USED THE SAME PLASTIC SURGEON

*Your fucking doctor has ruined
me,* Trump cries. He holds her arms.
Begins pulling out fistfuls
of hair from her scalp. Rips off
her clothes. Unzips his pants. Fucks
her. First time in sixteen months.
She runs. Hides. Locks door. Cries all
night. Comes back to the master
bedroom in the morning. Sees
her hair scattered on the bed.
He glares, asking, *Does it hurt?*

duly noted:

Harry Hurt III, *Lost Tycoon: The Many Lives of Donald Trump* (W.W. Norton, 1993)

In a statement given just prior to the book's printing and after her divorce was finalized, Ivana Trump said: "On one occasion during 1989, Mr. Trump and I had marital relations in which he behaved very differently toward me than he had during our marriage. As a woman, I felt violated, as the love and tenderness, which he normally exhibited towards me, was absent. I referred to this as a 'rape,' but I do not want my words to be interpreted in a literal or criminal sense."

Sunday, October 16, 2016

CFC HFC HRC GALAXY NOTE 7 SEE OH TOO

Let's hear it for Kigali!
Let's hug those sweating polar
bears but enough about them
let's remember us, riding
our rickshaws into rising
waves of engineered fish and
regret. Each smartphone longs for
165 pounds
of raw earth to make it sing,
times 2.5 million hot
Galaxies junked. Do the math.

Monday, October 17, 2016

THE RIGGING

The stays, the sails, aye, the ropes
and chains, the shrouds, the masts, spars
and yard of any fine ship
or coarse jumble of rotten
wood still afloat but off-course,
heading unknown, off the coast
of reason, works in concert
to move a floating body
from one harbor to the next,
safe from sea serpents, dark swells,
and outrageous octopi.

Tuesday, October 18, 2016

JULIAN ASSANGE CALLS TECH SUPPORT

Your call is important to
us. Please listen to our men-
u, as menu options have
changed ……………… Kenny G music ……………… Hi
Mister Julian thank you
for your patience. Let me see
if I can help you out right
here. Hmmmm, let me put you on
hold just briefly while I try
and see if I can fix your
problem ……………… Kenny G music …………………

for Chelsea Hadley

Wednesday, October 19, 2016

THE OCTAGON: ULTIMATE FIGHTING CHAMPIONSHIP: HE SAYS, SHE SAYS

HE SAYS

Inner cities = black.
Build a wall = xeno.
Elite bankers = Jews.
Voter fraud = excuse.
Locker room talk = TALK.
ISIS = my best chance.
Benghazi = Thank God.
Her emails = Thank God.
Stamina = pussy.
Latinos = new word.
Conspiracy = truth.

SHE SAYS

Building bridges = note
metaphor. Life in public
service = pain in ass.
Why am I doing this keep
smiling!!! You know = pre-
lude to folksy anecdote
indicating connection
to ordinary people.
No quid pro quo = Trump
voters don't do Latin. I
hope to earn your vote =

Thursday, October 20, 2016

CONGRATULATIONS USA! GO TEAM!

We made it through four debates (including Veep) without a single lonely hummingbird-fluttering, forked-tongue question about climate change. Best just to watch this dripping mass of manflesh sweat, sniff, gulp water—game show contestant who knows not the rules of the game—seethe there for all to gape: the most pussywhipped man in history.

duly noted:
http://www.politico.com/story/2016/10/full-transcript-third-2016-presidential-debate-230063

Friday, October 21, 2016

BEWARE DITTO MACHINES (BE THEY SIMPLE QUOTE SUBSTITUTES, RUSH'S SLAVISH DITTOHEADS, OR NEWLY-MINTED TRUMP SPOKESPERSON, JESSICA DITTO)

Back in camp, we used spirit
duplicators to print our
weekly newspaper. Who came
in what place in what sport, plus
the Moon landing. Fresh copies
in aniline purple pig-
ment were aggressively sniffed
and so would you. As they fade
in attic'd trunks and cardboard
boxes no doubt our aging
cancer chances grow higher.

duly noted:
https://www.donaldjtrump.com/press-releases/trump-campaign-statement8
https://www.donaldjtrump.com/press-releases/donald-j.-trump-for-president-campaign-announces-hiring-of-deputy-communica

Saturday, October 22, 2016

1,200 MESSAGES IN JOHN PODESTA'S
INBOX RE: ENERGY / CLIMATE

or

SHALL WE BE SCANDALIZED?
SHALL WE BE PLEASED?

Methane leaks, water tables.
Ethanol: mend it don't end
it. Can't alienate corn
country. Iowa. Bernie
fracking ban: unfeasible,
extreme. Stick a fork in it.
Halliburton loophole. Life.
Steyer. McKibben. Max flex
incrementalism. Green?
Have done extensive polling
on carbon tax. It all sucks.

Sunday, October 23, 2016

REPUBLICANS IN GETTYSBURG (CREATED EQUAL)

… -score and seven years ago
Every woman lied when they
our fathers brought forth on this
came forward to hurt my cam-
continent, a new nation,
paign. Total fabrication.
conceived in Liberty, and
The events never happened.
dedicated to the prop-
All these liars will be sued.
osition that all men are …

Monday, October 24, 2016

THINGS THAT WILL STAY THE SAME

King tides and the Moon's heavy
pressure. Corrosive rot on
free speech of money, money
being speech in our country.
Heartbreak a radish inside
my chest, past expiration.
The smell of rain in the air
before it rains. Excuses.
The babysitter next door,
who shouts on leaving, always,
"Love you, love you, little loves."

Tuesday, October 25, 2016

IT'S ALL DOWNHILL FROM HERE, BABY

So he goes and stops, and he
says, "Come on, baby. Come on,
baby." I went up. I went
two flips in the air, two flips
very near in front of him.
I disappear! Donald was
so angry, he took off his
skis, his ski boots, and walk up
to the restaurant. He could
not take it. He could not take
it. —Ivana Humpalot

duly noted:
http://www.nytimes.com/2016/10/26/us/politics/donald-trump-interviews.html
http://www.imdb.com/character/ch0002421/

Wednesday, October 26, 2016

A BLACK & WHITE LAD IN A NEWSBOY CAP WITH A SHARP VOICE FROM AN OVERHEAD ANGLE BARKS ON THE SIDEWALK (AS WE ZOOM TO READ THE HEADER) "HOT OFF THE PRESSES! READ ALL ABOUT IT! TYCOON TRUMP CAUGHT IN LOVE NEST WITH SIX PAPERS NATIONWIDE WHICH ENDORSE HIM! AFTERNOON FINAL! RUMORS OF A SEVENTH! READ ALL ABOUT IT! JUST TWO CENTS!"

Waxahachie Daily Light. St. Joseph News-Press. Santa Barbara News-Press. Antelope Valley Press. Times-Gazette of Hillsboro, Ohio. *The Las Vegas Review-Journal* of Sheldon Adelson. No self-respecting fish would be wrapped in one of these six sheets. The Magnificent Seven counting *The Enquirer.*

Thursday, October 27, 2016

HOW RICH: THE ROOTS OF THE FAMILY FORTUNE IN THE KLONDIKE GOLD RUSH WHERE THE DONALD'S DRAFT-DODGING GRANDDAD FRIEDRICH DECAMPED TO MINE THE MINERS WITH HIS EATING, DRINKING & SLEEPING ESTABLISHMENT

or

THE SAGA OF SURPLUS CAPITAL

Every Delicacy in
The Market Served claimed the ad
for the Arctic Restaurant.
That meant: Fresh Fruit … Ptarmigan …
Horse Meat … Girl Meat. *Fresh Oysters*
in Every Style. Private Box-
es for Ladies and Parties.
In the boxes, beds and scales
for weighing payments in gold
dust for the hollow chambers,
the dark places of women.

duly noted:
https://open.library.ubc.ca/collections/bcnewspapers/bensun/items/1.0314940#p4z-3r0f

Friday, October 28, 2016

RAINY MORNING ON BREITBART

CORRUPT ESTABLISHMENT lede.
Human hand grenades tossed through
windows of the One Percent.
Hillary coffee (DECAF,
WEAK, BITTER) mug shots sold. Rape
jokes. FREE online courses to
get the skills you need to land
the job you want (Supply Chain
Management). Clinton Plan To
Strip Religious Liberty
Protections. POLLS: NECK AND NECK.

Saturday, October 29, 2016

BLACK SWAN EVENT

Former Miss Finland Ninni
Laaksonen and former Truman Scholar Moira Smith had
their asses firmly fondled
by, respectively but not
respectfully, Donald Trump
and Justice Clarence Thomas,
Trump because she looked like a
pre-pregnant Melania,
Thomas because he wanted
her ... to sup right next to him.

for Dr. Kimberly Washington

duly noted:
http://www.law.com/sites/almstaff/2016/10/27/young-scholar-now-lawyer-says-clarence-thomas-groped-her-in-1999/
http://talkingpointsmemo.com/livewire/miss-finland-ninni-laaksonen-trump-groping-allegation

Sunday, October 30, 2016

ELECTILE DYSFUNCTION

We last saw Carlos Danger
in late March, adrift on his
raft of crotch-shotted spoiled sheets.
Weinergate rhymes with penis
the way Watergate rhymes with
torture and lets not forget
Whitewater where Comey was
Deputy Special Counsel
to the investigating
Senate Committee. Quick send
in the clowns. Don't bother they're …

duly noted:
see March 28, 2016, "THE BLACKER THE BERRY, THE SWEETER THE JUICE" and a titular cameo on August 30, 2016, "ONCE AGAIN, WE VENTURE INTO HUMA ABEDIN AND THE CROTCH OF WEINER"
http://www.cnn.com/2016/07/07/politics/who-is-james-comey-fbi-director-things-to-know/

Monday, October 31, 2016

TREAT OR TRICK?

Don't you just love that our race
for the country's top job spins
on the whirred gyroscopic
perversions of three spooky
men—D. Trump, B. Clinton, A.
Weiner—who think with their dicks?
Now, imagine a world run
by women, where the first man
within sniffing distance of
the prize was pushed out by sexed-
up Kegeling amazons.

Tuesday, November 1, 2016

THE CALL HAS FINALLY COME

I'd been waiting, swarthily,
through this whole impossible
election season. Waiting
for the word. Waiting to take
action. The three-note ringtone
on my burner phone (JEW-S-
A, JEW-S-A) awoke me.
A man with a faint Euro
accent, speaking from the crypt
of a shadowy central
bank, spilled my marching orders.

duly noted:
http://fusion.net/story/321668/trump-star-of-david-tweet-hillary-clinton-excuses/
http://www.newsweek.com/2016/11/11/donald-trump-companies-destroyed-emails-documents-515120.html

Wednesday, November 2, 2016

DRAIN THE SWAMP (THE POLLS TIGHTEN)

Raised on television and
revenge, we just might get our
plot point right: someone to rule
us so brutally stupid
and ostentatiously id-
norant we don't feel so dumb
no more. You can't have a beer
with him since he don't drink but
you can feel he's one of us:
a walking, shouting realtors'
comp for the slum we live in.

Thursday, November 3, 2016

THE ENTHUSIASM GAP

What is it about this baked
potato of a woman
which provokes such loathing or
meh, icky acceptance? She
laughs, folks cringe. She speaks purple,
people see red. She hits Send,
off with her head. The other
guy could shoot someone on Fifth
Ave—as he mimed it—his gang
would vote for him ten times each.
She manages half a vote.

Friday, November 4, 2016

TRUMPISM IN THE LAND OF LAFAYETTE, JEFFERSON, AND WASHINGTON

Fascistic Republican-
ism is the new black. We
sink or swim with ink spilled, marks
made in the booth we fought for.
Blood. Kin. A couple hundred
years of unpaid labor. Hey
neighbor. The far right digs a
beachhead against the rising
tide of a majority
minority nation. Young,
scrappy and obese, we flail.

for Daveed Diggs

Saturday, November 5, 2016

MICROTARGETING (SWING STATE SCRIPTS)

If I was a Pacific
Islander/eager Asian
American my *Call Tool*
would have fed me to Friday
night Nevada phones needing
company, but my knowledge
of Manzanar and hula—
sketchy, lame. The Woman-To-
Woman script begged reading for
Colorado, but last I
checked I'm short a uterus.

Sunday, November 6, 2016

THE MARGIN OF ERROR

Inside the chalk lines lazes
the margin of error, sprawled
on the grass, under the late
fall sun. In his tattered bag,
he squirrels charts and crystals, a
cigar and a banana
for the coming cartoon slip,
mirror-bright microchips. Chips.
Diminishingly small, we
are an edged sum, rounded down.
Every shut eye ain't asleep.

Monday, November 7, 2016

SAY IT LOUD—I'M WHITE AND I'M PROUD
("GET ON THE TRAIN" FBI REMIX FEATURING
JAMES "SHORT BOY" COMEY, SPECIAL GUEST
H.H.W.A. *HARDBALL HONKEEZ WIT ATTYTUDES*)

Some people say we got a lot of malice
some say it's a lot of nerve I say we won't
quit moving til we get what we deserve we've
been 'buked and we've been scorned we've been treated bad
talked about as sure as you're born oooweee you're
killing me alt-right you're outta sight so tough
you're tough enough ooowee you're killing me oow

for Ron Miles

duly noted:
https://www.youtube.com/watch?v=RBVVztMA4CQ
https://www.youtube.com/watch?v=2VRSAVDlpDI
http://www.jango.com/music/James+Brown

Tuesday, November 8, 2016

NAME, ADDRESS, PHONE

Noel Ali. Phyllis Pyles.
Mimi Violin. Lucas
Miles. Misty England. Michael
Gentile. Alma Soria.
Ricky McGill. Mary Guy.
The names, the beautiful names
of Americans. I tried
to reach you, but couldn't. Now
we must put away trifling
toys, the empty candy of
entertainment, and choose best.

Wednesday, November 9, 2016

EIGHT YEARS AFTER OBAMA

a whitelash, with wicked torque.
For every action, equal
and opposite reaction.
Pale men and women without
college just changed the course of
this country for good, and bad.
Not tactics: plate tectonics.
Not farce: tragedy. It's real
hot and will get hotter. This
goes well beyond words. It is
done. It is done. We are done.

for Ofelia Diaz-Guzman

CAMPAIGN: KUDOS

Thanks bigly and yugely to Marc Vincenz, who morphed a blog into a proper book. His patience, perseverance, and commitment to getting things right is a model for any Campaign Manager. Cheers, man!

Thanks to Adam "Red Dog" Blitz, who, crucially, gave me the time and space to make this happen: without him, no 7-Elevens.

Thanks to Brad Swift, Nels Cline, Mary Halvorson, Mark Dresser, Matt Merewitz, Norman Atkins, Chelsea Hadley, Ron Saint Germain, and Barbara and Don Ruhman, loyal readers of the blog who provided needfully noisy feedback on the daily dispatches.

Thanks Beth Anderson, Ryan MacGavin, Chris Sacco, and Don Katz at audible, for giving this book a voice.

Thanks to Amit Majmudar, Deborah Garrison at Knopf, Danny Lawless at *Plume* and Herb Leibowitz at *Parnassus* for shining light on some of these 7-Elevens before they came wrapped in these covers.

Thanks to Nicole Miller for helping me finesse ABC to XYZ cover designs.

Thanks to my best, earliest editors, who taught me concision, never use two when one would do: Bob Christgau, Sears Jayne, Michael S. Harper, Peter Balakian, Keith Waldrop, Robert Wallace: a complete and total wrecking crew, who built me.

Thanks to my kids, Billie Miro and Thelonious Blue, for *dealing* and understanding why I often was scarce at breakfast and beat during "put downs"....

Last, and above all, thanks to Isabel Breskin for her inspiration, kind guidance, random idea generation, and co-piloting skills: she was often in the right seat (throughout the bumpy flight) while I was in the left.

db
17 April 2017
San Francisco

CAMPAIGN: ACKNOWLEDGMENTS

My thanks are given to the editors of the following publications, where these poems previously appeared:

Resistance, Rebellion, Life: 50 Poems Now (Knopf, 2017):
  Mountebank

Plume:
  A Very Artful Smear
  Scalia in Marfa
  The Bridge and Tunnel Crowd
  Pyroclastic Flow
  Let's
  Visceral / Not Visceral
  Republicans at Gettysburg (Created Equal)
  Treat or Trick
  Trumpism in the Land of Lafayette, Jefferson and Hamilton

Parnassus: Poetry in Review:
  Culture of Complaint (Donald's Victimization Department)
  Plans for Altering the Desert: Sonoran Border Wall
  GOP Cartoon
  Mountebank
  Look at My African-American over Here:
      Look at Him! Are You the Greatest? *(June 5, 2016)*
  Look at My African-American over Here:
      Look at Him! Are You the Greatest? *(June 6, 2016)*
  Populism
  Fact-Check
  Storm Surge (Matthew 28:19)

ABOUT THE AUTHOR

Born in Chicago in 1958, David Breskin first made his name in the 1980s and early '90s as a freelance journalist, writing for national magazines such as *GQ, LIFE*, and, most prominently, *Rolling Stone*, where he was a contributing editor. Breskin covered a wide range of cultural figures—Willie Nelson and Bono, Miles Davis and Martin Short, Michaels Jordan and Jackson—and authored high-profile investigative pieces on teen suicide, murder, and mayhem.

After publishing a novel, *The Real Life Diary of a Boomtown Girl*, Breskin turned away from journalism and toward poetry, and by the mid-1990s had begun publishing poems in *The New Yorker, The Paris Review, Parnassus, New American Writing*, and *TriQuarterly*, among other periodicals. His first book of poetry, *Fresh Kills*, was published in 1997, and his second, *Escape Velocity*, in 2004. Between those volumes, he created and edited *RICHTER 858*, a multimedia inquiry into the abstract paintings of Gerhard Richter, with music by Bill Frisell and contributions by thirteen American poets. His next work, *Supermodel* (2007), was a one-sentence epic poem, or novel-in-verse. More recently, Breskin conceived and produced *DIRTY BABY*, which married his sixty-six ghazals to sixty-six pictures by Ed Ruscha and music by Nels Cline. He has also published a book of interviews with film directors, *Inner Views: Filmmakers in Conversation*, which features dialogues with Francis Coppola, David Cronenberg, David Lynch, Spike Lee, Oliver Stone, Robert Altman, Tim Burton, and Clint Eastwood.

Breskin has also worked as a record producer for the past thirty-five years and, in addition to Frisell and Cline, has collaborated with leading-edge musicians beginning with John Zorn, Ronald Shannon Jackson, Vernon Reid, and Joey Baron in the '80s and early '90s, and continuing with Mary Halvorson, Kris Davis, Craig Taborn, and Chris Lightcap in the current decade.

Breskin lives in San Francisco. Most of his work may be found at davidbreskin.com.

CAMPAIGN: A NOTE ON TYPE

The text of *Campaign* is set in Caslon, the invention of William Caslon (1692–1766), an English type designer. Working initially in London as an engraver of ornamental designs on firearms, Caslon set up his own foundry in 1716 and debuted his typeface in a 1734 broadside. Caslon is cited as the first truly English typeface—English printers prior to this time used mainly imported Dutch types. (Caslon himself based his type on Dutch models.) Originally produced exclusively by H.W. Caslon & Company, the type was widely distributed throughout the colonies of the British Empire, including those in North America. The rough look of early American printing can be partially attributed to the effects of oxidation on the metal sorts, which were exposed to seawater during the long voyage across the Atlantic. Caslon faces were used for most important printed works in English between 1740 and 1800, including the first printed version of the United States Declaration of Independence. Caslon is characterized by bracketed serifs, moderate modulation of stroke, and some resemblance to Venetian antiqua letter forms. Among other things, George Bernard Shaw said, "I'll stick with Caslon until I die."

The display face of this book is set in Kremlin, designed by Vic Fieger in 2005. Born in 1982, Fieger is a contemporary designer, illustrator, gadfly, maker of comics, and typographer, who has authored fonts across the spectrum: stencil, handwritten, erosion, techno, and faux-foreign. Kremlin is of this last category, and Fieger describes it thusly: "El Lissitzky was the Russian designer whose multitude of book covers popularized the concept of Soviet typography being presented in grid-based monoweight letters with dominant right angles. His best-known piece is *The Red Wedge*. The letters in Kremlin were inspired by Lissitzky's works and followed a grid of 4 squares by 5." Fieger also writes passionately on the subject of Russian design: "If you'd like to learn more about Russian constructivism, you can probably do that." Much of his work can be found at vicfieger.tumblr.com.

www.ingramcontent.com/pod-product-compliance
Lightning Source LLC
Chambersburg PA
CBHW040315170426
43196CB00020B/2923